Praise for MERGE

"Bill reminds us that 'selling' is much more than presenting a product to a prospect—it's a disciplined process. Ignore the process and risk being marginalized by your clients and reduced to bidding wars with your competition."

—David W. Bensinger
V.P., National Director of Sales
Executive Benefits
Lincoln Financial Distributors, Inc.

"For too long, insurance professionals have forgotten to talk to client needs in client language, and to clearly explain the value proposition and product offering. To some, buying insurance has become an illustration game. The MERGE Process goes a long way toward avoiding these pitfalls."

—Robert J. Hebron
New York Life

"If you want to succeed in the financial field, MERGE is your bible. Bill articulates 30+ years of success into clear, concise formulas to benefit readers regardless of experience level. He takes the glut of theories and conventional wisdom on how to sell and distills it into an ethical, modern process to improve consulting skills and results."

—Philip E. Steele, President, AIF®
Pension Architects

"Forget everything you know about marketing and business building and "MERGE" into an unconventional path to meaningful success. Industry legend-Bill MacDonald-gives you the most powerful and instructive business building manual you'll ever read."

—Moe Abdou, Founder
The Koenig Group Wealth Management

"Bill is truly one of the finest marketers and salespersons in the country. Even after running my own successful company, I found piece after piece of valuable advice in MERGE. I will recommend it to others without reservation."

—Jack Dolmat Connell, Managing Partner
Dolmat Connell, Executive Compensation Consultants

"Great advice from the industry veteran Bill MacDonald."

—Eric Flaten
Financial Advisor

"Bill shares the secrets of the super successful salesperson in MERGE. No stone is left unturned. Famed UCLA basketball coach John Wooden used to profess "mastering the basics" and "controlling the controllables"—that's what Bill does in MERGE. Make it a priority read."

—Simon Singer, CFP®
The Advisor Consulting Group
Past President International Forum

"Most people who write about marketing don't grasp the nuances of what elite life insurance agents do for a living. Bill's insight and credibility jumps off the pages as you realize the depth of his experience with sophisticated buyers."

—Bob Carter, Founder and President
Lion Street Independent Life Advisors

"Problem solving versus solution selling—by applying a clear collaborative selling process you can effectively maneuver through the company's decision making culture, while bringing all decision makers into account. Bill MacDonald exploits this process in spades with common strategy in an uncommon manner. MERGE should be required reading in every graduate school and advanced underwriting curriculum."

—Michael J. O'Donnell
Alliant

"Whether you're considering financial services, young in the industry or a mature executive, learn from MacDonald as he shares those techniques that have made him one of the most successful intangible consultants in the past 20-years."

—David A. Bardes
David A. Bardes Organization, Inc.
Founder, Clark Bardes, Inc.

"Bill MacDonald has consistently earned seven figures year after year by being a consummate professional. The Merge Process reveals his unique system of research marketing and collaborative selling. Written in a simple, clear and succinct manner, anyone can learn Bill's system. MERGE is a roadmap for success that's well worth studying."

—Stan Fidel, President
Fidel Communications Co. Inc.

"After 40 years in the financial services business, I thought I'd seen and heard it all about selling financial services.. I was wrong. Bill MacDonald's book MERGE is the best treatise available on becoming a superior sales person. He covers all the bases and encapsulates in one book the many talents and techniques of those at the top of our industry. If you intend to be among the best of the best in this industry, you need to read, study and follow the MERGE Process."

—Peter F. Hibbard, CLU, ChFC
Columbia Benefits Consultants, Inc.
Board Member, The Forum 400

"MERGE is a must read. Bill is the most persistent new business and relationship/account builder I've ever known, and I see thousands in my line of work. If you want steak and not sizzle, this author and this book are difference makers for anyone serious about profitably growing their businesses."

—Bill Bean, Founder
Strategia

"The MERGE Process emphasizes hard work and preparation, not some faddish silver bullet that will instantly double your sales. Because Bill MacDonald focuses time-tested, immutable interpersonal and communication strategies and a keen understanding of human nature, this book will remain valuable to the financial and professional services for years to come."

—Michael S. Melbinger, Partner
Chair, Employee Benefits & Executive Compensation Practice
Winston & Strawn LLP

"Our business pursues a mission to help customers succeed financially by protecting what they value most. MERGE offers practical guidance to drive our insurance and risk management professionals to new heights of performance. Apply Bill's straightforward insight and boost your worth to clients now."

—Neal R. Aton, President & CEO
Wells Fargo Insurance Services, Inc.

"Bill MacDonald's new book lets the reader in on the marketing and sales secrets of a legend in our industry. He's giving back to us a formula to keep our businesses growing and inspire us to new heights with great techniques to win and keep clients."

—Steven C. Price, CEO
Solenture, Inc.

"MERGE is a must-read for anyone with a new or established career in financial services. Better still, it's the only marketing/sales playbook you'll ever need to do well in our business."

—Robert Birdsell, Managing Director
RCG – Milwaukee

MERGE

MERGE

Simplify the Complex Sale in Five Surefire Steps

How Hard-Charging Consultants in Professional
& Financial Services Slow Down to Succeed

by William L. MacDonald

authorHOUSE®

AuthorHouse™
1663 Liberty Drive
Bloomington, IN 47403
www.authorhouse.com
Phone: 1-800-839-8640

First published by AuthorHouse 6/20/2011

ISBN: 978-1-4634-1784-0 (sc)
ISBN: 978-1-4634-1783-3 (hc)
ISBN: 978-1-4634-1785-7 (e)

Library of Congress Control Number: 2011909774

Printed in the United States of America

TABLE OF CONTENTS

ACKNOWLEDGMENTS

I could not have written MERGE without the input and support of many others. I would especially like to thank Carolyn L. Smith, Magnus & Co., with whom I have worked throughout my career. Her knowledge of sales and marketing and passion to write about it has been a valuable asset to each of my firms, and to me personally. Carolyn pushed my thinking forward during all stages of this book, acting as my agent, editor and collaborator.

This book is the result of many people and experiences across 30-plus years' of business. It began when I entered professional services as an executive search consultant with Lan Goodwin in Worcester, Massachusetts. Lan was my first view of a true professional on top of his game. As a young recruiter, I was exposed to financial services, and developed a keen interest in the sale of insurance products. Along the way, I had the opportunity to join Bob Fine's team at Guardian Life, and work with some great people at Connecticut Mutual including Dave Ford and Tom Meehan.

Through my involvement with the Young Presidents' Organization (YPO) I made best friends in the membership and benefitted from new ways of thinking. A special thanks to my YPO forum. YPO also exposed me to its program at the Harvard Business School, where I learned strategic thinking from some of the best resources in the world, and built a competitive advantage as I developed the tools to look at my industry much differently.

Over the years, I have also been fortunate to form relationships with key advisors considered experts in their fields—Arthur B. Laffer, Paul B. Fay, Dann Angeloff, Charlie Lynch and others. I especially wish to thank John Buckingham, marketing professor at Pepperdine University, for his advice and help on expanding certain topics.

Of course, my deepest appreciation goes to those former Compensation Resource Group, Inc. (CRG) associates who shared their knowledge and experience with me, especially my partners Bill Forrest and Keith Tobias who were there from the beginning. I learned from every member of our team, and thank them for their dedication to building a world-class firm.

My former associates at Retirement Capital Group helped me keep many of the concepts we discuss in this book fresh and exciting. Special thanks to Amy Ripplinger, Chris Olstad and Natalie MacDonald for their edits and illustration work that pulled everything together.

Above all, I express my deepest gratitude to Eileen, my lovely wife of 40 years, to my son Bill Jr., and to my daughter Natalie for limitless understanding of my long hours and obsession with business.

PREFACE

*"The key to this business is meeting people under
favorable conditions."*

I first heard these words 30-plus years ago from Bob Fine, my general agent with the Guardian Life Insurance Company and one of my first sales managers. Early on, he taught me the importance of positioning yourself to be perceived as an expert by your prospect. I fused this lesson to my brain and built a system around it that integrates sales and marketing in a process-driven approach. Along the way, I booked hundreds of millions of dollars in revenue in the financial services industry.

Thousands of books on sales and marketing fill the shelves of American businesses. What makes this book different?

First, MERGE is focused solely on business-to-business (BtoB) sales and marketing of professional and financial services, one of the most difficult industries to master. Services are intangibles and much harder to sell than manufactured products. Financial and professional services are complex and challenging for buyers to understand. Practitioners seem to hide behind obscure knowledge and speak from strange lexicons. Add to this the issue of trust: How do you trust what you cannot yet see or understand?

MERGE lays out both sales and marketing strategies to teach you a selling process for better control of your sales cycle. It shows you how to use research to uncover critical business issues so that your client sees you as a trusted advisor instead of another salesperson.

As you'll soon learn, the MERGE Process is about problem solving, rather than product sales. Think of it this way: Business problems are like mice; they go unnoticed until they start nibbling at your cheese. Yes, you could build a better mousetrap, but that may not be a big enough differentiator to inspire the world to beat a path to your door. And people who don't have mice, or don't think they have mice, won't be interested in your mousetrap—until the mice show up. Then, when they finally feel the nibbling, you had better be circling that cheese with your mousetrap.

MERGE shows you how to position your firm, stand apart from competition, get recognized as an expert, and even engage others to help you land the sale. What's more, I will lay out the marketing and sales foundation to establish your business model. Best of all, MERGE teaches you what to do after the sale to keep your client engaged in the relationship.

While most business books on sales or marketing focus on one or the other, very few merge the two. I know from hard-fought experience that you need to work hard to be more than good enough at both. In marketing, companies must develop and execute effective go-to-market strategies to create and exchange value with clients. In sales, companies must engage in specific problem solving and collaboratively bring that value to clients. Otherwise, everything comes to a standstill.

Today, the marriage between marketing and sales, if there ever was one, has outgrown its traditional vows. The web and social media have catapulted clients to the front of the sales cycle where they can easily research products, services and options with the investigative insight of Sherlock Holmes. Armed with deeper knowledge, prospects, clients and customers today ask tougher questions. In my business, they pull in procurement departments, issue RFPs, and shut down opportunities to present self-serving, canned presentations. It is increasingly difficult to reach higher level decision makers in a prospect organization. Clients at all levels have plenty of choices and never want to be sold.

Against this backdrop, the seeds of MERGE took root, producing a repeatable, easy-to-follow process that removes the lion's share of guesswork in selling services. With MERGE, marketing and sales naturally line up, like a pilot's flight safety check before he prepares to fly his aircraft.

I developed the MERGE Process to help meet the challenges of the changed environment we compete in today. Like you, I have studied a myriad of marketing and sales approaches. Most approaches were centered on solution selling. What worked before doesn't work today. Even the word "solution" has worn out its welcome.

When Bob Fine coached me on positioning, I made the decision to go up-market and sell bigger ticket items to larger and more sophisticated buyers. I knew the competition would be tough and I knew the sales cycle would be longer. But I wanted to make the investment because I also knew the rewards were limited only by my commitment. As the MERGE Process evolved, I made mistakes, and in the process I learned lessons. One outcome was constant: When my consulting team followed the process, we won. When we took shortcuts, we failed.

Another early mentor told me that I "needed to do certain things to be successful, the things unsuccessful people weren't willing to do." At that point, I decided not to take my vacation in 15-minute increments. And now, I guarantee, if you invest the time and effort into the MERGE Process, and are willing to do what others are not, your rewards will be limited only by your commitment to succeed.

INTRODUCTION

I am an entrepreneur. My business of choice is financial services. Growing companies is my passion. In my four decades of business, I have hired hundreds of intelligent, hard-working, motivated individuals to serve as salespeople and consultants to help grow my companies.

I was always frustrated with how often they confused activity with results and sold product features and benefits rather than the value proposition we had to offer. Many of these consultants appeared to be doing everything right. They were personable, displayed excellent communication skills, and had solid knowledge of our business and products. Most were also good listeners. What's more, my staff armed them with field-proven proposals that typically delivered results.

Yet with all these qualities and tools, they didn't win the business. Like me, they were frustrated because their hard work did not produce more income. I kept asking myself what was the big difference between those who succeeded and those who failed? Were the successful people simply lucky? Did they have better contacts? Did they work harder? Did they play the numbers game?

In fact, the successful ones called on fewer people than the unsuccessful consultants; however, they simply exerted greater control over the selling process. At a cellular level, they understood the difference between activity and results and sold the value proposition, rigorously following the MERGE collaborative selling process.

Let's recreate a typical sales call to illustrate.

John, our consultant, targets a "profile prospect" (based on predetermined criteria such as motive and means to buy). Next, he does some background research, often limited to a current proxy, annual report or website, and learns enough to ask some penetrating questions at an initial meeting. The prep work seems to stop there. Although our consultants are urged to do thorough research, they often avoid the process, preferring to rely instead on rapport building skills. John then schedules the first meeting.

INITIAL SALES CALL

Let's review the conversation as the meeting and follow-up unfolded.

Consultant:	"Good afternoon, Bob, I really appreciate you giving me the time to meet with you today. How has everything been going?"
Prospect:	"Pretty good, John. How has your business been?"
Consultant:	"It's been real busy with all the recent changes in the tax law. I know the economy has been a little bad for some people recently—how's your business?"
Prospect:	"Everything has been fine. We have actually been growing and expect to have another good year."
Consultant:	"Well, I know you're busy, so let me get down to business. As you know, I'm with XYZ Company. Our principals have been in business for more than 35 years, and we have seven regional offices, including the one here in Los Angeles. We're proud to be the executive compensation and benefits consultants for several companies in your industry. We would like to also have an opportunity to work with you on some of the issues you may be dealing with. With whom do you work now?"
Prospect:	"We've been with ABC Benefits for five years, ever since they merged with Milton Consulting. They handle our nonqualified deferred compensation plan."
Consultant:	"How has it been going with ABC Benefits?"

Prospect:	"Fine, no real complaints."
Consultant:	"Any problems with the service they provide?"
Prospect:	"Not really anything to speak of."
Consultant:	"How many people are in the current deferred comp plan?"
Prospect:	"We have 170 eligible participants, with about 50 people participating."
Consultant:	"Why do you think participation levels are so low?"
Prospect:	"I really don't know. I am personally in the plan and think it is fine. I know we haven't promoted the plan as much as we did when we first put it in. I know a lot of the new participants are spread out in different locations, so they may not be getting that personal touch people receive from ABC Benefits here at headquarters."
Consultant:	"I see. Any concerns with ABC's ability to service those people in your remote locations?"
Prospect:	"No. They've done a good job. It might be more on our side. I don't think we want to spend the extra money to reach out to them."
Consultant:	"How are you funding the plan? Are your fees for administration paid separately?"
Prospect:	"We have set up a rabbi trust, and we are funding it with life insurance. The administration fees are separate."
Consultant:	"Has anyone done a review of the life insurance products since you put them in? New products have come out with much lower cost to the company, and often with the capability to save the administration cost on top of everything."
Prospect:	"No we really haven't done that. We are depositing $2 million annually based on the amounts of deferrals, and I have never really had a good understanding of how the products actually work."
Consultant:	"Bob, I'd like to put together a proposal that shows how we can improve the company's profit and loss statement and eliminate the extra cost for plan administration. If we can potentially save

you some money, maybe as much as $200,000 in year one, is there any reason why we can't do business?"

Prospect: "No, not at all. We'd be happy to receive a proposal from you. Just let me know what data you'll need and I will get it to you."

John left this meeting feeling energized and followed up by sending Bob a data request form. John received the data a few days later and began working on the proposal; John also sought input from a senior consultant on how best to show the results, using his meeting report.

When I asked him how the meeting went, he said Bob didn't really have any issues with ABC Benefits, but his company was very interested in cutting costs and improving their P&L impact. In fact, he was quite excited; the data proved we could produce first year savings closer to $300,000, rather than the $200,000 he told Bob in the meeting.

FOLLOW-UP MEETING

John completed the report/proposal and met again with one of our senior consultants to optimize the report and personalize every aspect, complete with prospect logo. The presentation shined. Follow-up day arrived:

Consultant: "Thanks for having me back, Bob. We processed your data and are pleased to present our findings in this report. In fact, we uncovered even more savings for you than anticipated; we found another $100,000 in the first year alone."

Prospect: "Sounds good; let's see what you have."

Consultant: "As mentioned, based on the total annual premium, we can improve your first year profit and loss by $300,000. Better yet, over the first 10 years the savings would be $810,000. What's more, we can eliminate the annual administration fees you pay to ABC Benefits for even greater savings—another $32,000 a year for plan administration. With all of these savings, what do you think?"

Prospect: "Well, John, this is very impressive. I had no idea. I really never understood the insurance funding. We'll definitely consider your

	proposal. Let me spend some time reviewing this report, and I will get back to you."
Consultant:	"Bob, based on these savings, do you see any reason why we can't take over your deferred compensation plan?"
Prospect:	"John, I like the results you have come up with, but we have a tendency to move a little slowly around here; however, I promise we will take a serious look at this."
Consultant:	"Thanks, Bob. Why don't I call you back in a couple of weeks? Maybe we can get together and review this report in greater detail. Then I can answer any outstanding questions."
Prospect:	"That sounds good, John. Look forward to hearing from you."

I ran into John after his meeting, and he was visibly enthused. He and Bob, the CFO, had a "great" meeting and John claimed to have "great" rapport with him. Further, John said Bob was pleasantly surprised at how much he could save with us. John saw no reason why Bob wouldn't adopt our recommendations. The improved numbers would make the sale, or so he speculated.

What John Didn't Know

As was customary at year end, CFO Bob reached out to his contact at ABC Benefits. He asked straight out what ABC Benefits could do to reduce the cost of insurance funding for his deferred compensation plan. The consultant immediately sensed something was up.

When he pressed the question, Bob said he was considering a change because one of ABC's competitors had shared a new, savings-driven product. First, however, Bob wanted to see what ABC Benefits could do, before he switched. They agreed to meet.

ABC Consultant:	"Bob, I appreciated your call to me last week. Your business means a lot to ABC and to me personally. As you know, our team has been dedicated to servicing your account, and we are always there for you when you need us. I don't know who you have been meeting with, or what they have been telling you,

but I'm sure we can improve the cost of your funding and be as competitive on fees and cost as anyone.

"With this enrollment, we anticipate plan growth that will give us access to products unavailable when we first began the relationship. As you'll remember, we put in a lot of time and energy getting this plan started, and now that it is growing, there is a lot more we can do. If we can produce some savings for you, do you see any reason why we can't continue our relationship? We will do whatever it takes to keep your business."

Prospect: "You guys have done a great job for us. We are focusing on cost in all areas of the company. If you can help us in this area, we will have no reason to leave. Believe me, I know how much work it was in putting in the original plan."

ABC Consultant: "I'm sure we can do that Bob. Thanks for your confidence in us."

A few days later, John called Bob on the phone as he had promised. He was still quite excited, feeling that his proposal produced economics no one could turn down.

Consultant: "Bob, did you have a chance to digest our proposal?"

Prospect: "Yes. You were very thorough, and I want to thank you for going through the trouble of digging into our data and producing the report.

"I shared the report with our director of human resources and the vice president of benefits, who does the day-to-day work on the plan. They were both impressed with the report and your services, too.

"I guess it comes down to timing, John. We are just so busy with a number of projects right now, and no one has the time to focus on this. HR is going through the re-enrollment of our health and welfare plans, and I'm in the middle of budgets, and I need to get ready for our annual shareholders' meeting. Our current provider, ABC Benefits, was already scheduled to review this area with us, and has come up with similar savings. So based on all of this, it's something we can't deal with right now."

Consultant:	"I understand, Bob. Let me suggest that I stay in touch, and maybe I can come back out after the first quarter and spend some time with you and your team, when people have some of the projects off their plates."
Prospect:	"That sounds great, John. I think our timing may be much better."

Next Move

John entered all of this data into salesforce.com, our CRM system at the time, reminding himself to call after the first quarter. In my weekly meeting with John, I asked him the result of his call to Bob.

John explained, "It seems like Bob and his group are tied up on a number of projects and couldn't find the time to focus on this now. Also, they spoke to ABC Benefits, and they said they could also produce these savings. I still think Bob must be asking himself why they didn't bring these savings to him before. I think we're in great shape. He asked me to call after the first quarter."

John had focused on product features and benefits and did not convey the value he could create for the CFO and the company. Most of us were taught the FBA (features/benefits/advantages) method of selling. FBA centered on your ability to memorize feature details and translate them into client benefits. The best salespeople used this simplistic approach to align client interest with the benefits being sold: "This is what I have; this is why you need it."

In John's case, he assumed the CFO was pre-motivated to change vendors, based on cost savings alone, which was a shortsighted and premature judgment. This tendency is a major problem with many salespeople today. They find a great prospect, and when there's an inkling of receptivity, they go directly to the product sale and usually pitch something around cost savings. They jump to a solution too quickly. That's comparable to locking all the exits in an overcrowded theater.

An ideal initial approach for John would have been to open the meeting with a series of questions formulated around his in-depth pre-research of the prospect's company. That approach leads naturally to a collaborative process in which understanding of prospect issues takes priority.

As you will see later, the collaborative selling process begins by asking questions in a purposeful mode. You will learn where John made his first mistake. Had he followed the process, he would never have led by inquiring what product or service or current vendor a company uses. The process never leads to a feature or benefit selling point without first determining whether there is a need. Although these are common sales openings, they do not build a solid relationship with your prospect. You need to ask more engaging questions, identify areas of mutual opportunity, and position yourself as a consultant with a genuine interest in the prospect. Only then will the prospect be more receptive to your ideas and recommendations.

As we will discuss later, it is foolish to build sales strategy around price or cost savings alone. Although John did some research and had a decent understanding of the prospect plan—even getting Bob to send confidential plan details—John's process ultimately did not differentiate the offering enough for Bob to switch. Even $300,000 in savings could not dislodge the incumbent. John overestimated Bob's reaction. In fact, Bob said he really never understood how the funding worked.

John underestimated the depth of the relationship with ABC Benefits. He should have known Bob would give ABC a chance to match his offer. No one wants to "rip up the sidewalk" and switch vendors until they absolutely have to. The current provider, no matter how bad its services may be, will get another chance to bid, unless the prospect clearly sees and internalizes the difference in value.

When there is complexity in what you sell, the competitive advantages become blurred in the client's eyes. By applying a clear collaborative selling process, you can effectively maneuver through the company's decision making culture, while taking all decision makers into account.

John failed to differentiate XYZ from ABC Benefits. He mentioned only in passing that XYZ maintained local presence through its regional offices nationwide and offered decades of business experience with blue chip clients. He did not identify meaningful differences between XYZ and its competitors—nothing that convinced Bob to switch. As a result, he never had anything to sell other than a price difference and a willingness to improve funding and plan administrative cost. Importantly, this example doesn't change if you're selling other types of financial products or professional services.

In this book, I provide you with a marketing and sales process to advance every sales opportunity and increase your closing percentage. Most sales books teach you sales tactics; I honestly do not believe in tactics. I do believe in professional services that merge sales and marketing, so you are well positioned and have the right collaborative selling process to get the job done.

Always remember that prospective clients do not want to be sold. They want you to understand their business and their issues and help them solve their problems with an effective collaborative process that they can readily understand and accept. I must warn you in advance, it is not a quick sales process, and it is not breakthrough thinking.

What is it? Do the common things uncommonly well, and follow our Five-Step MERGE Consulting Process.

I have written this book to pay it forward. Consulting in financial services has given me freedom and success beyond expectation. If by sharing what I've learned, I can help shorten your learning curve to greater income, then I've fulfilled an important personal mission. Please read on.

William MacDonald, *President*
PleinAire Strategies, LLC
San Diego, California
June 2011

1 | Everyone Sells

Everything Changes

Practically everything we do involves some form of selling. Asking friends for dinner. Requesting a credit line extension at the bank. Changing financial advisors. And all selling, by its nature, anticipates (even expects) some sort of change to occur.

Someone will buy our product. Someone will upgrade to the premium version. Someone will refer our service. Someone will switch competitors. Someone will pay us for what we do. Selling is the commercial spine of society. Without it, the muscles of the economy would freeze up and atrophy.

But people generally dislike change. And don't want to think they're being sold. Yet selling is an honorable profession. I relish the quote, "Nothing happens until something sells," a derivative of the classic Einstein statement, "Nothing happens until something moves."

Consider that 34 gigabytes of content moves through the American mind every day. More than 100,000 words march past our curious eyes and ears in a single 24-hour period. Where did these bytes and words come from? People generating ideas, thinking, doing, selling.

To be sure, we exist in an enormous, undulating bubble of pure sales energy anchored by a web of communication channels ranging from television, radio and the web to simple word-of-mouth exchanges. In reality, change is the DNA of selling.

AT THE GATES OF COMMERCE

But has selling changed to reflect our over-communicated lives? After all, the Internet has leveled the playing field. Prospects can do all their homework online, comparing competitive offerings quickly and easily, until points of differences virtually disappear. While consumers commoditize, we the sellers of services scramble for higher ground. We've become a nation of well-armed, well-informed consumers. And consumers are at the gates of commerce, in charge and in control.

In the words of satirist Ben Stein, "Sales—when done right—is more than a job. It is an art. It is a high-wire act. It is, as Arthur Miller immortally said, being out there 'on a smile and a shoe shine.'"

Assuming your Cole Haans are polished and your pearly whites are showing, what do you need to succeed in sales today? What does it take to surge to the top? What skills are required to perform at the peak of this challenging and honorable profession?

THINGS CHANGE

Historically, the selling of financial and professional services has been a product sale, bound up with hard-closing techniques and the earmarks of a high-volume transaction. Offer a product. Find a ripe client. Price it right. Ask for the order. Close and move on.

Now in the era of financial planning—assets under management, fees for service and value perceptions—the selling of financial and professional services most often rises or falls on trust, which is not now, and never will be, a commodity.

The ability to sell sustainably is governed by direct and indirect influences. Direct influences include the disciplines of methodology, procedures, tools, systems, metrics and structure—what I call the atmospherics—which propel activity through the pipeline with the energy of a well-defined, replicable process to mold every engagement into a result, a sale. This process flow is essential to longer concept sales such as executive compensation and benefit solutions.

Indirect influences, or the softer skills, are the most difficult to achieve in a climate where the public trust has eroded. During these times, outstanding sales producers must rank even higher in authenticity, authority, rapport-building, credibility, likeability and emotional intelligence—characteristics that engender trust, which we address in detail in subsequent chapters.

Many thousands of books have been written on what it takes to surge to the top in sales. Certainly, trustworthiness is at the top. And while I may not add a new nugget to the pile, I can offer a quick composite of the qualities I observed working with successful sales leaders mano a mano.

Sales Leader Snapshot

- Expertise in business operations
- Grasp of business trends
- Impeccable knowledgeable in the niche
- Deep understanding of prospect need
- Authentic likeability factor
- Mastery in forging relationships
- Adept at nurturing lasting relationships
- Skill to balance behavioral differences of multiple decision makers

I have discovered that the very best don't just sell products and services or solutions, and they don't berate the competition trying to sell similar concepts. They choose to play at a much higher level by identifying previously unidentified opportunities. Most of all, they create value and added solutions to their client's situation. In turn, they achieve significantly higher levels of success than others. And they use all of the characteristics mentioned above.

KEEP IT SIMPLE

To succeed in sales today, you must form relationships with executives at the top of the organization and meet them under favorable conditions. Understand how top executives think and what they need so you can communicate relevant information and provocative ideas. And you must be positioned well, with a marketing strategy that is consistent with and complements your sales process.

Keep in mind that in complex sales, we are dealing with busy people, who are overwhelmed with many pressing issues. Overwhelmed people can't take in, sort through, or make sense of massive amounts of data on products and services they can't see an immediate need for. You must communicate with these decision makers in a simple and straightforward manner and stay focused on adding value by helping them to resolve an issue or achieve a goal.

The business of sales is no longer a numbers game. Things have changed:

- Simplicity has recently emerged as a major factor in sales success
- Prospects see you as irrelevant if you present information about your products and services or solution before you understand their business and its challenges
- Technical presentations are out and value creation is in

I have witnessed many salespeople present three- to four-inch proposals with tons of data on their products features and benefits, only to learn it is the fastest way to extend the sales cycle or to lose the opportunity completely. You will be far more successful making fewer high-quality calls, meetings and presentations.

If you asked 100 different sales managers what they look for in sales leaders, no doubt you'd hear 100 different answers. My list is only a snapshot and jump-off point to the Grand Prix in 21st century selling—*agility to respond with perpetual change.* There is only one way to respond with perpetual change, and that is to master the MERGE Process, and bring together sales and marketing for a shorter sales cycle.

The MERGE Process reduces risk, improves quality, permits experimentation, drives sales, and manages change. In upcoming chapters, I am going to help you develop and follow a straightforward process for marketing and selling financial services—or any type of professional service—that produces repeatable results and creates a place for client trust to grow and sustain itself.

It is a deceptively simple process that has made me millions of dollars.

It will for you, too.

2 | Dare to Differentiate

Setting Your Firm Apart

The financial and professional services industry constantly wrestles with the numbing sameness of commodities. From insurance to investments and planning to advisory, products and services quickly blur before the eyes of the average buyer because there is no real differentiation from one offering or one advisor to another.

"A commodity is simply a product waiting to be differentiated," claims Professor Philip Kotler, a world-class thinker on marketing. Ask a consumer why he buys one term insurance product over another. Ask another why he relies solely on his company 401(k) plan and does no supplemental investing on his own. Ask a small manufacturing company why it does not offer an executive benefits program, even though this is a proven, sure path to competitive advantage. For some, it is a question of cheapest price. For others, it is lack of time to understand the product. For many, the differentiated value was never explained clearly.

Failure to Value

In one revealing study, 40 percent of 200 buyers of consulting and professional services admitted that service providers did not understand their needs; 32 percent claimed the service providers did not convince them of the value they could expect to receive from the service provider.

In Chapter 6, we discuss the core value of research and preparation for your initial client meeting. An essential key to a successful meeting is how clearly you understand the value gap or pain point felt by your client and whether your product or service differentiation eases that pain.

Professor Michael Porter of the Harvard Business School in his book *Competitive Advantage—Creating and Sustaining Superior Performance* proposes that though a firm can have a myriad of strengths and weaknesses vis-à-vis its competitors, there are two basic types of competitive advantage a firm can possess: low cost or differentiation. These elements, combined with the scope of activities for which a firm seeks to achieve them, lead to three generic strategies for achieving above-average performance in an industry: cost leadership, differentiation and focus. The strategy has two variants, cost focus and differentiation focus. The generic strategies are shown in Chart 1.

CHART 1

COMPETITIVE ADVANTAGE: THREE GENERIC STRATEGIES

		Lower Cost	Differentiation
Competitive Scope	**Broad Target**	1. Cost of Leadership	2. Differentiation
	Narrow Target	3a. Cost Focus	3b. Differentiation Focus

Source: Michael E. Porter, *Competitive Advantage*

Pulling from Porter's thinking, I'll summarize his key points going forward. Cost leadership is perhaps the clearest of the three generic strategies, wherein a firm sets out to become the low-cost producer in its industry. The firm is broad in scope and serves multiple industry segments, and may even operate in related industries. Firm size typically shapes its cost advantage.

The origins of cost advantage depend on industry structure and take many forms. They may include economies of scale, proprietary technology or better access to raw materials. How you cost out the value of an activity is often subject to economies or 'diseconomies' of scale. Economies of scale arise from an ability to perform activities differently, more efficiently, and in greater volume. These economies also capture the ability to amortize the cost of intangibles such as R&D, money management, accounting services or client administration, and also over greater sales volume.

Diseconomies of scale are often present in many financial and professional services, which are dependent on fast-response times and creative individuals who may not perform well in large organizations. To achieve cost leadership, one must carefully examine every aspect of firm activity, look for opportunities to reduce cost, and then pursue of all of them on a consistent basis.

The second generic strategy is differentiation. In this strategy, a firm works on a unique position in its industry as defined by, perceived important by, and valued by buyers. As the firm meets client needs, it is rewarded for its distinctiveness with a premium price—only if it is truly unique at something or perceived as unique. Differentiation can be based on the product itself, the delivery system by which it is sold, the marketing approach, and a broad range of other measurable factors.

The third generic strategy is focus. This strategy is quite different from the others because it relies on choosing a narrow competitive scope within an industry. The firm selects a segment or group of industry segments, then tailors its strategy to serve those segments only. By optimizing its target strategy, the firm can build a sustainable competitive advantage.

Using Porter's framework for financial and professional services, once you have defined your differentiation as he suggests, there are only three ways your firm can show competitive advantage:

1. **Exclusivity.** Offer a product or service no one else has the capability to offer, and then communicate its value with conviction and repetition. Recognize that product differentiation is difficult to sustain as competitors copy and eventually improve on your value. Know, too, that product differentiation is often unnecessarily complex, full of jargon and technical terms. Be absolutely sure you do not confuse the client with all the extraneous glitter,

the bells and whistles, or he may miss your exclusive offering altogether.

2. **Process.** It is not enough to do most things a little better than the competition. You can, however, gain advantage by how you deliver your service or produce your product. Differentiate with a process that helps you explain that "it is not what you do that makes you different, but how you do it that gets better results for your clients." Use selected references to increase the credibility of your statement differentiator.

3. **Value.** Distinguish your value proposition. When your product or service is similar, find a competitive advantage based on the effectiveness of your value presentation. Explain it in a clear and compelling way, and motivate your prospect to take action. This can be accomplished when you thoroughly understand prospect issues and clearly articulate your value proposition.

Accountants, brokers, consultants, executive recruiters, financial advisors, and lawyers can all appear the same in each vertical niche. Each may offer roughly the same services for about the same price. If a client believes your products and services are essentially the same as everyone else's, he can exert tremendous downward pressure on price. I see this reality frequently in financial services because financial instruments are not easy to understand.

Clients tend to oversimplify the decision process to overcome the perceived complexity of the choice they face. This is inevitable when you lead with a product instead of a focus on client needs. Simply put, the product is not the thing—mutual fund insurance, accounting, law—it is the process for solving the client's needs.

DEFINING VALUE

Your value proposition is precisely how you differentiate. And there are hundreds of points of value in business offerings. We define a value proposition as the offering that describes the quantifiable benefits received from buying your product or service. It is created by a review and analysis of the benefits, cost and value that an organization can deliver to its clients.

Neil Rackham, the author of *SPIN Selling* believes that a value proposition statement should consist of four main parts: Capability, Impact, Proof and Cost. Capability is what you do and how you do it. Impact represents the benefits or differences your capability will make. Proof is what evidence substantiates your impact. Cost is the cost (or risk) of your capability and impact. See Chart 2 below.

CHART 2

VALUE PROPOSITION

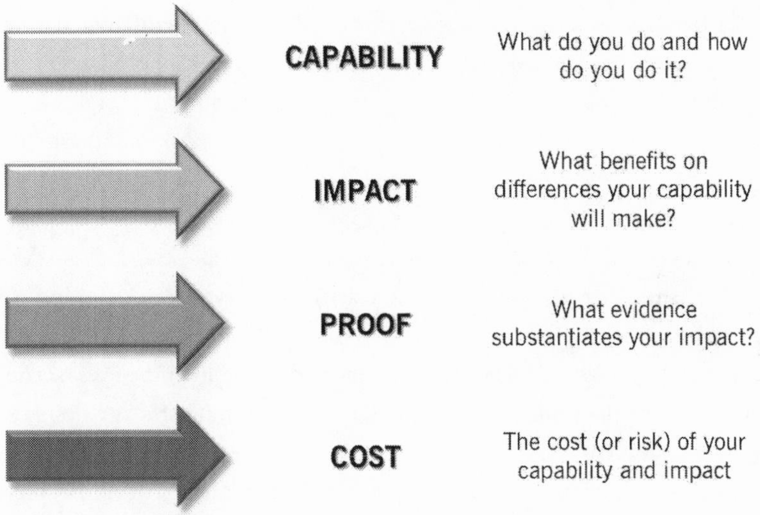

→	**CAPABILITY**	What do you do and how do you do it?
→	**IMPACT**	What benefits on differences your capability will make?
→	**PROOF**	What evidence substantiates your impact?
→	**COST**	The cost (or risk) of your capability and impact

Source: Neil Rackham, *SPIN Selling*

You may differentiate value on communication, customer service, your process or consistent delivery of results. You may differentiate on efficiency, exclusivity or flawless execution, but you must be able to prove it, and demonstrate the impact it will have on your prospect. The creation of a value proposition is part of your strategy. Your value proposition is your firm's internal blueprint to ensure that all of your marketing messages are consistent, inside and outside of your organization.

Well-regarded consultants Michael Treacy and Fred Wiersma refer to value disciplines in differentiation. You can aim for product leadership, operational excellence or client intimacy, for example. You can position and differentiate around a key attribute, benefit, application, or category. Other possibilities include:

❏ Best quality	❏ Best performance
❏ Most reliable	❏ Most convenient
❏ Safest, fastest	❏ Best value for the investment

MORE FOR LESS

Kotler breaks down five value propositions that define themselves by their names: More for More; More for Same; Same for Less; Less for Much More; and More for Less. Today, given the intense pressure on price, service firms may be well advised to adopt a *more for less* positioning and emphasize differentiation around proof of that *more*. If successful, you could eventually justify premium pricing, or more for more.

Whichever point of differentiation you choose—and can prove—demonstrate it to your prospect with the clarity of an eye-clean diamond. In this way, few, if any, competitors can authentically appropriate, duplicate or outright steal what makes you different and valuable in the eyes of your prospect. Your firm must also adopt a value positioning strategy designed for your target market.

I am continually amazed in my business travels when I ask people I meet, "What is your firm's point of differentiation?" Strangely, I often get a blank look in reply or, even worse, a stutter and an awkwardly uncomfortable response. It's a simple question, "So what makes your firm different from others?"

Take some quality time to think critically about differentiation. Develop a dynamic list of specific areas in which you excel. It may be the hard probing of your research department; the trust-selling style of your sales force; or the way your receptionist never forgets the voice and name of a new client. It may be the completeness of communication materials to clients; your skill at solving intractable problems or even something as simple as how you volunteer in the community.

Don't underestimate anything, because an action that appears simple to you may be the one thing that sets you apart from the competition. Become your own best knowledge center and continually strive to get fresh answers for the basic questions:

- *What do your clients really appreciate about your service?*
- *Why are long-standing clients still with your firm?*
- *What are some of the best testimonials shared by clients since you began your business?*

When my organization went through the exercise to determine our value proposition, we concluded it was "not what we did but how we did it that made a difference." Our firm's capabilities and process produced predictable client results, thus eliminating surprises. Our client references speak to that differentiator and provide the proof. Our firm's research process provided us the information to identify to clients what impact they could expect. We share our research approach, a critical step in the MERGE Process, in chapter 5. We will discuss how you can sell this approach in chapter 7.

The challenge for service firms is to make the differentiator completely *visible* to the target prospect, well before the purchasing decision occurs. Marketing expert Harry Beckwith calls this *The Invisible Touch*. The ability to reach out and help a prospect make a decision based on the experience of the product or service *before* you put it in her possession is nothing short of miraculous.

SEE IT, BELIEVE IT

Imagine you are in a mid-life crisis. The only solution is a new motor-cycle. You know next to nothing about bikes, so you go to a nearby dealer. Suddenly, around the corner, you hear the unmistakable "potato-potato-potato" sound of the exhaust of a beautiful Harley-Davidson V-twin Road King. You're toast. You sign the contract—an invisible touch.

Now, you're on a road trip with that move-outta-my-way Road King, you pull into a café and, wafting out of the kitchen, is the smell of blueberry cobbler. You're overwhelmed with memories of Mom and stop what you're doing to call her. Ah-h-h. You feel better.

Soon, you're back at the office, still nursing midlife heebie-jeebies and, out of the corner of your eye you spot the tip of a sailboat mast peering out from the pile of magazines and mail on your desk. Your eyes can't stop looking at it. Before you realize you are on the phone to your travel agent to book that long dreamt of Windjammer trip to the Galapagos. (Midlife crises are expensive).

Well, you get the idea. Sight, smell, sound, taste and touch. Appealing to a prospect's five senses is characteristically tough when selling services; however, it is a personally satisfying way to differentiate your product or service.

The invisible hand of experiential marketing accelerates your prospect toward a decision because it allows him to more clearly understand outcomes—when he signs the elective deferral document, $200,000 more fills his pocket at retirement and gets him aboard a Windjammer to the Galapagos with nary a care.

STAND OUT

To stand alone, you must stand out. Here are four tips toward differentiation, if you dare:

1. Create hard-to-ignore offers by wrapping your package in irresistible value
2. Become the acknowledged expert in your discipline; act and give as a thought leader
3. Develop a clear process to the client's situation, and develop a solution in a collaborative manner to make the client's situation more predictable
4. Give clients the added value of convenience with access to you 24/7 via email or IM

Whatever you do, do not differentiate on price; it is a fool's game played by people who never learned you must do what the unsuccessful people refuse to do. Who really wants to be the cheapest? People flock to higher-priced products, stay at five-star hotels, and buy luxury-brand names. Why is this true? The answer is clear: Top-of-the-line products possess value. Or, at a minimum, they are perceived as more valuable.

The notion that you get what you pay for proves itself millions of times a day as American consumers scramble to get a deal. But cheaper can evoke perceptions of lower quality, less reliability, even unstable business environments.

I recently listened to a radio spot for a UCLA educational program which extolled, *"If you think excellence is expensive, wait till you get the bill for mediocrity."*

Value Above All

We all face competitors who turn an opportunity into a price-bidding war. When I face this challenge in our organization, I always try to get the client to give up some of the valuable service I am proposing, rather than reduce the price. As an example, we offer plan design; plan documentation; financial analysis of funding alternatives; a complete investment analysis with a registered investment advisor (RIA); enrollment and education using chartered financial counselors (CFPs) working with the participants; monthly financial reporting for the company; 24/7 access to web tools; a dedicated client team; and research on new tax law changes. The client can quantify the potential savings with each element of the service.

We lock in our success when the client recognizes we provide much more value versus asking us to reduce the price, especially if that reduction is less than the company's actual cost savings. In a recent client engagement, I suggested we work closely with the client's legal counsel. He could supply the plan document, and the company's current registered investment advisor could design the investment menu and eliminate the use of certified financial planners in the enrollment process. This recommendation would result in a 25 percent reduction in fees. The client recognized the value and decided to pay our fees.

In short, when we listed out all of the services and broke down the price, the client clearly understood the other competing firms did not provide equivalent value. In fact, the general counsel of the client company discovered his outside legal counsel intended to charge nearly 80 percent of our total fee for the plan documents alone!

In another situation where price became an issue, we designed a performance-based contract. We were so sure we could increase participation and save the company millions of dollars that we offered to reduce our fees if we failed.

TAKEAWAY

As of late 2008, the Investment Company Institute factbook lists 8,022 U.S. mutual funds to choose from. More than 650,000 financial advisors do business in America, across thousands of advisory firms, representing an immeasurable number of individual stocks, bonds, REITs, futures, annuities, bank CDs, and private placements. Little wonder people need to turn to "experts." But which expert goes to the heart of differentiation. Will it be you?

Let's end this discussion with a quick four-point takeaway on differentiation:

1. Carve out a riveting value proposition to bring to life your point of differentiation
2. Build a distinguishing process of doing business that you can replicate to perfection
3. Clearly communicate with every client points showing how you solve tough problems
4. Master of the art of discovery by knowing your prospects and clients better than anyone

3 | YOUR GO-TO MARKET STRATEGY

Organizing Your Approach

Many businesspeople confuse sales and marketing, often using the words interchangeably. Worse yet, marketing and sales teams frequently fight over turf, leaving each other clueless about their respective disciplines.

Selling begins at the point of product launch, while marketing begins well before. Think of a bridge: On one end stands the salesman; on the opposite end stands the client. Marketing is the entire bridge: towers, pylons, cabling—all of it. For the salesman to reach the client to ask for the order, companies build the bridge and pay the toll.

Philip Kotler, regarded as the foremost expert on the practice of marketing, explains it best: "Marketing is the art of creating genuine client value. It is the art of helping your clients become better off. The marketer's watchwords are quality, service, and value." Okay, we know "nothing happens until something sells," but this is only once you know your market, what clients need, and what they'll pay for.

LACK OF PLANNING

Marketing is as much a process as consulting. It begins with the development of a sound marketing plan, and then unfolds as a series of simple actions with predictable results. In time, a well-implemented marketing plan expands your client list, market reputation and firm value. Surprisingly, fewer than 32 percent of the best financial advisory firms have created a plan, and only half of those have implemented it, according to a 2010 readership study by Financial Planning magazine. In professional services, Robert Half Legal found that 83 percent of law firms offer formal sales and business development training to their lawyers, however, few have a formal plan.

Your firm creates value by how you market. It sounds simplistic, but that value is created when you meet a client need. Let me repeat, value is created when you meet a client need. If we agree that a firm cannot define itself by the product it sells, only by the differentiated value it creates for the client, then we have common ground to lay down a go-to market strategy.

Let's recall the sales call example from the introduction. John assumed his prospect was ready to buy his product based on the cost savings to the company, but the CFO did not see that value because the incumbent matched John's product and price.

While cost savings is a good value proposition, John didn't communicate it in a definable way to show he was bringing more value. He uncovered cost savings to improve the company's P&L, but it wasn't different and the CFO didn't see the value (impact) it had on his organization. The incumbent could do the same, and did.

John went directly to the product without framing all of the issues and getting the client to agree with the value gap. If he was focused on cost savings, he could have broadened the scope beyond the deferred compensation plan, explaining the impact it would have on the company, his capabilities, then proving how he could do it with case studies and professional examples. Without the benefit of research, he would not uncover the possibility of a better approach to show his value added. Good value propositions ultimately produce outcomes a client can tangibly grasp in advance—higher revenues, lower cost, reduced employee turnover, improved client retention, or greater operational efficiency—all quantifiably proven.

Value as Market Strategy

Your ability to demonstrate your point of differentiation; that is, the measurable value you bring to the client—determines success. And it can only be defined from the client's perspective. You may add an interesting feature or benefit to your service that, in your opinion, screams value, but if the client doesn't care about it, it is not value-added. To understand value, ask these basic questions:

- Why do clients choose certain solutions and/or sources of services?
- What current cost and drivers dictate their behavior?
- What would cause them to change behavior?
- What unmet or poorly met needs do they have?

Your existing clients are your best source of defining value because value is defined in their minds and from their perspective. Spend time with them and ask what they value, you may be surprised. The only way your firm can justifiably charge premium pricing for your products or services is by creating real value in the client's mind and on his balance sheet. For example, what you do for the client may empower him to outperform a competitor and grab market share. It may save sufficient resources to allow him to hire needed staff, open a new facility, or fund a blue-sky project. Your firm must continuously improve on and enrich your offerings, which is how you create sustainable value and the framework for your marketing strategy.

THE TARGET MARKET

Begin by selecting a target market. Do you want to serve only those individuals with investable assets over a particular dollar amount? Do you want to serve only technology companies with revenues in excess of $100 million? Do you prefer to handle only qualified plans, insurance or estate planning for a selected market? These are decisions only you can make, based on your skills, resources and market demand.

When the target market is clearly defined, your firm is able to make intelligent investments in marketing, and select the best vehicles for reaching the desired audience. As we will see later, everything you do with your go to market strategy, including your website, will center around your target market.

A word about segmentation. In most markets, there are unlimited ways to segment, and I suggest you spend adequate time on this process. Study and understand all aspects of your market demographics, regional characteristics, buyer psychographics and, in particular, behavioral finance, which seeks to identify how and why people make financial decisions.

MARKET POSITIONING

Determine how you want to position your products or services in the client's mind. Are you the first to market with a new idea? Are you the logical alternative to a competitor? Are you the safe decision? There are many ways to position your product or service vis-à-vis your competition. Above all, be credible and be prepared to defend your position with believable facts.

Be creative by communicating a position that is simple, powerful and memorable. To get it exact, write your positioning down into a compact paragraph, as little as one or two sentences. Keep at it until the language lifts off the page and raises the hair on the back of your neck.

Once your positioning is clear, it is time to develop your value proposition. Jack Welch, former Chairman of General Electric, said, "The value decade is upon us. If you can't sell a top-quality product at the world's lowest price, you're going to be out of the game . . . the best way to hold your clients is to constantly figure out how to give them more for less." Remember our discussion in chapter 2, a value proposition statement should focus on four key elements: capability, impact, proof and cost.

Ask yourself, how will my client experience the value of my service? As more for less? As the gold standard? As the innovative leader? As full service? The most trusted? Preferred brand? Once this critical step is committed to paper, and you can prove it, create a plan for the marketing activities needed to achieve this desired positioning.

Once you select your target market segment, position yourself and define your value proposition, you are halfway to your go-to market strategy. You are also in the process of defining your brand. You can follow the core Five Cs (Chart 3 below) to develop your go-to market strategy by asking yourself:

1. **Client**—What need does our target client have that our firm seeks to satisfy?

2. **Company**—What special core competence does the firm possess to meet those needs?

3. **Competition**—Who competes with the firm in meeting those needs? Take your blinders off, and look at direct, indirect and substitute products or services.

4. **Collaborators**—Who should the firm enlist for help; how do we reach them; and how do we motivate them to act in our favor?

5. **Context**—Which cultural, technological and legal factors limit our abilities to accomplish all of the above?

CHART 3

MARKETING ANALYSIS – THE FIVE Cs

Client	Company	Competitors	Collaborators	Context
What needs do we seek to satisfy?	What competencies do we possess to meet those needs?	Who competes with us in meeting those needs?	Who should we enlist to help? How do we motivate collaborators?	Which cultural, technological, & legal factors limit our possibilities?

1. & 2. Analysis of Client and Company

Our first two Cs deal exclusively with matching what your client needs with what you offer. Ben Shapiro, one of my favorite Harvard professors, says simply, "You need to start with the customer." [Companies refer to both clients and customers; we prefer clients who buy services versus customers who typically buy commodities.] Identifying and understanding your client is a critical first step. I will assume you have identified the end user of your product or service as your client, which might not be the case if your services are sold through intermediaries or direct or indirect sales forces.

Most successful service organizations zero in on a specific market rather than apply a scatter gun approach to marketing to avoid squandering limited resources and time. This segmenting step helps define client value perceptions and organizes your selection of target clients, which resources to apply, and even how you exploit the weaknesses of your competitors. Let's review some basics:

- **Demographics:** For example, high-net worth individuals with estates over $100 million; occupations such as doctors or executives; publicly traded companies over $100 million in revenue and, in general, education, household income, net worth.
- **Geographics:** Narrows your focus by selecting national, regional or zip code-specific local communities.
- **Lifestyle:** Offers insight into patterns in consumer behaviors in such areas as finance, travel, shopping or preferences such as hedonistic vs. value oriented.

Once you select the target prospect, stretch your thinking to fully understand needs and value expectations before building your value proposition. Be sure the value proposition is one that supersedes the competitive offer. As discussed earlier, the value proposition represents the economic, strategic and operational value of benefits promised to clients to meet their unsatisfied needs. To achieve a strong value proposition, firms need to master knowledge of their targeted client base. By identifying client needs through research, firms develop and better communication clear and concise value propositions to reflect those needs.

At this stage, you must also look to your company's resources to make sure you can deliver the value your client seeks, which is why we discuss the two Cs (Client and Company) together. Examining client value can cause a major shift in your thought process, especially for those of you who are product salesmen. Each client applies a different set of values to reach a buying decision. When you truly grasp this, you will achieve the first step in value segmentation.

Value segmentation helps you to easily classify your best clients and find more like them. By targeting them, you can tailor your communication to capture their attention, thus improving the likelihood they will do business with your firm.

Take the example of a firm in the retirement planning business that decides to segment the market based on size of client organization, number of employees, and asset size of retirement plans. It can target companies with 500-2000 employees or with pension assets of $5 million to $15 million. But its explicit choice of a target market defines the services and resources required to meet the client expectations. Each client segment dictates the value sought, the price paid and, essentially, the rules of engagement.

In Chapter 3, we discussed how you can differentiate your firm based on the value-driven consulting process it uses. Again, it is not **what** you do, but **how** you do it (a process) that brings true value to your client. A well-designed process produces better results for clients, creating a more predictable outcome.

Consider the example of a California-based retirement service company that targets the 401(k) plans of mid-size organizations with 5,000 to 15,000 employees in such high-turnover industries as restaurants, construction companies and call centers. The company's value proposition is built on its communication and educational strategy surrounding the plan enrollment process. It demonstrates to clients how to increase participation levels, which helps the company be more competitive, without increasing cost. The firm can show the impact this competitive edge will have on the company's profitability by showing the value of reduced turnover. To win over prospects, the CEO refers to her clients who substantiate this value proposition, her proof, without increasing cost.

Understanding the Client Buying Process

As you select your target market and understand what it values, study the buying process your client undergoes. Do you understand how he makes a purchasing decision? For our clients, the purchasing of professional or financial services is a process, not an event. Therefore, it is essential to adapt a marketing and selling process to match their decision making process. It is also essential to understand who will directly or indirectly influence the client decision.

The buying process usually begins with an initial discussion of a value gap, identified earlier by you. At this point, the client is beginning to experience a problem, but may not be ready to act. Based on his initial experience, the client may begin to think and perhaps more actively explore what change might mean for his situation. To gain more information, the client may reach out to its law firm, accounting firm or another trusted advisor. He or she will even use the Internet to search for information. In chapter 7, you learn why compelling website content is a magnet to draw prospects into the sales cycle.

CHART 4

CLIENT BUYING PROCESS

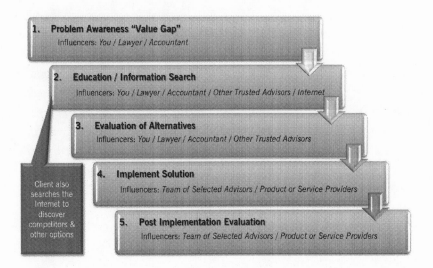

As clients begin to commit to resolving their problem and evaluate the alternatives, they start to focus on building a case, perhaps looking to other advisors in your field. These advisors will all become influencers. See Chart 4.

Ask yourself how the influencers fit together. Does any one person carry greater weight? Who are the gatekeepers, the technical or economic influencers, the possible champions? Map out the buying process around your value proposition for a visual representation of how companies make decisions. Test it. Verify it. Update it. Refer to it often.

For instance, imagine the case of Jason B., a life insurance agent who provides estate planning services. His products are normally sold via a trust, depicted in the buying process [Chart 4], and provide a certain level of tax planning and peace of mind to his ultimate client. Jason's choices in strategy, trust type and funding are influenced by a lawyer, an accountant, the trust company, and the insurance company. Although not directly part of the purchasing process, these influencers can make or break his sale, as can the IRS regulations that must be satisfied. Note Jason's solution at the beginning of the buying process. Each person in the sequence can add value to your products and services, but you must identify them early and design a collaborative process to bring them into the client's buying process.

Jason wants to provide his services to high-net worth individuals with estates in excess of $50 million. His challenge is to learn how his prospect goes about analyzing, deciding and implementing strategies to deal with the tax issues he faces.

At some point a client will consider whether he needs to purchase financial products and services to deal with his issues. Clients want to understand their options and not be sold on one solution; they look for objective advice.

Jason needs to understand how he can fit in with the clients' other advisors to bring value. For Jason, it could be in the evaluation process. He could provide the client with education and a process for evaluating the issues and the magnitude of the problem. Knowing the client's buying process, he can play an important role in organizing the team of advisors. By reaching out to the trust officer, the lawyer, the accountant and other advisors early, he can limit the later surprises that invariably slow down the sales cycle.

Each member in the buying process holds his or her own set of needs and value expectations, which links into other members with desired benefits. The trust company cares about the rating of the insurance company and enhances Jason's product; the accountant is concerned with cost and can help the client and Jason understand product impact on his situation; the lawyer worries about the knowledge and experience of the agent in complex trusts, and can provide the legal documents to assure the client buys Jason's product in the most advantageous way.

To pinpoint these client value segments, begin at the deepest level in the buying process where your offering is recognized for its value and work back from that point, all the while discovering client value segments at each level up to the direct client.

CHART 5

SWOT ANALYSIS

Strengths	Weaknesses
Opportunities	Threats

LOOK INSIDE

Now that you've looked inside the prospect company, take an insider's view of your own. Analyze your firm's strengths, weaknesses, opportunities and threats (SWOT) in light of your segment competition [Chart 5]. Do a SWOT analysis on your competition, too, but be objective. Confront the immediate opportunities and threats. With all the change in the marketplace, there may be many challenges. Then examine how your strengths and weaknesses line up. Evaluate historical financial returns in the segment. Know what other advantages or disadvantages may occur when you jump into the space. Determine if your findings match your goals.

Be completely honest with yourself. If a midsize pension planning firm targets companies with pension assets over $250 million, it better possess the resources to compete with the major players in the space, knows its differentiators, and understands how to communicate earned value. Also, be sure that everyone in your firm buys into the positioning. Here are a few questions to help you rally your team onto the same positioning page:

What is the single most important claim we can make as a firm?

You may have multiple claims, and that is fine, if your claims are clear and supportable. To illustrate, one firm I work closely with provides medical insurance services to mid-market companies. In its marketing collateral, it states, "We bring Fortune 500 solutions and services to mid-market companies." The company practices Fortune 500 processes run by key employees who built track records at large consulting firms or in human resource positions in Fortune 500 companies. This firm has defined its market and organized resources around it.

What truly sets us apart from our competitors?

The medical insurance firm above implements a wellness approach to improve the health of client employees and demonstrates its success by lowering the client's cost of claims. To further differentiate itself, it offers the experience and credentials of an Executive Vice President of Wellness on staff, a position typically found only in Fortune 500s or large consulting firms which service Fortune 500s.

This firm often uses a client experience to make its point. For example, take the case of the mid-market company with higher than normal medical claims, which were driving up cost. Through its wellness approach, the company offered a premium plan with no deductibles for those who would take a blood test. This step allowed the program to better measure members' current health and set up a plan to improve it.

As part of its wellness program, the firm helped its client set up an exercise facility and succeeded in getting the client to remove the junk food from vending machines and replace it with fruit. This approach created the classic differentiation. These actions lowered claims and improved cost, resulting from added value, not selling the insurance product itself.

What is the single most important support we provide to our clients?

Adding to its wellness approach and process, our medical firm established a call center to fully accommodate all the inquiries resulting from its clients' medical plans. Remember, this is a mid-size company investing in proactive delivery of a high-touch service, quite remarkable for a company its size. As part of this service, it uses a special concierge service, which reaches out to the spouses of upper management to help them facilitate filing of claims. Again, demonstration of classic differentiation.

3. Analysis of Competition

With the third C, competition, there are several schools of thought: 1) Ignore the competition and concentrate on dominating your niche with superior product, service and performance; 2) Ignore the competition at your peril, and pay the price of a costly end run. Both contain nuggets of truth.

Of course, there are companies that have succeeded in their niche with steely focus on only what they do well, wasting precious little time on competitive intelligence, one-up marketing or displacement selling; for example, Google drug stores or cable operators with exclusive regions.

We all dream of breaking out of commodity markets, but the natural evolution of a maturing market eventually leads to commoditization. This is exactly why you must continually carve out a differentiated position, value proposition, hard-to-mimic process that somehow sets you apart. So it pays to pay attention to what your competition is up to—not to duplicate, but to distance your firm from the copycats in business.

In my long experience, I've taken comfort in knowing what my competition was doing, if nothing else, so I could outdo them. The irrepressible American spirit of competition is what makes business interesting and lively.

Exploit the Weakness

With this said, I recommend you identify both the current and potential competitors for your products and services in your targeted market. Understand their strengths and weaknesses as you keep differentiating. Maybe one competitor is undercapitalized, another understaffed, another lacking in new ideas. Whatever its Achilles' heel, exploit it without yelling "fire" in the theater.

Keep your eye on indirect competitors who could be potentially more annoying, if not precarious. A company in a mature market is more likely to be upset by a new entry disrupter than an existing competitor. My main threat comes from bundle retirement providers, which currently have only a small-market share, but I see them coming.

There are many tools available to conduct a sound competitive assessment. Be mindful not to lose touch with what is really important to your prospect. Remember, there are typically three ways to effectively differentiate yourself and your firm from the competition:

1. Offer an exclusive product or service with immediately discernable value. If you can deliver what no one else can, product differentiation, typically very hard to sustain, will define your market appeal.

2. Provide a way of doing something better than anyone else, a process that cannot be easily duplicated. You can then defensibly state that it is not what you do, but how you do what you do that produces better results for clients. Add to this the references of delighted clients, and you own a compelling sales argument.

3. Communicate your value proposition more clearly and more persuasively than anyone else. If you are up against a me-too competitor, you can gain an advantage by how well you present your services.

4. Tell your story on a well-constructed communication platform. Be creative, consistent and clear. Coordinate all your marketing and sales materials around the same powerful message, and you

are more likely to motivate your prospect to take action in your interest. Certain salespeople stand out and gain competitive advantage on their own individual presentation talents, and not entirely from the firm.

COMPETITIVE ADVANTAGE

A few years ago, I spoke at the International Forum to a group of the top two percent of salespeople in the world in the financial and insurance industry on the topic of competitive advantage.

In advance of the speech, I researched the group by conducting a survey. My team contacted 25 firms and asked the question, "What is it that gives your firm a competitive advantage?" Essentially, I wanted each firm to explain why they were different, knowing that most people jump right in and discuss products and services. Without exception, every firm claimed people, reputation, knowledge of its business, access to certain products, and great service. Even when we probed further, respondents did not offer any differentiation or specific competitive advantage. It may have existed, but they did not explain it to us in a convincing way. The results were somewhat surprising, given the caliber of the firms.

I continue to take this tack when I meet salespeople. Amazingly, most salespeople cannot explain with conviction how their offering differs. Some look at me blankly and say, "What do you mean?"

Thankfully, there was a standout salesman who told me, "It's our customer service." When asked to explain, he said, "At our company we don't have voice mail. A client reaches someone 24-hours a day, directly. Our phone systems transfer the call directly to our customer service team member's cell phone, and someone is always on 24-hour call. Also, all emails are received by all members of the customer service team simultaneously, and we have a first response policy."

And finally he said, "Our service department is not organized to be a profit center; it's there to service the products and services we sell. We do whatever it takes to satisfy our clients, and quantify our economic impact on their business. Customer service is baked into our culture."

That is differentiation you can understand.

4. Analysis on Collaborators

Inexplicably, some business people fail to network. Fear? No time? No energy? I've watched at events or meetings as these same people consciously or otherwise overlook the importance of building and maintaining collaborators who can help open doors and pre-condition prospects. That's why I crusade for an influence-building strategy around the fourth C, collaborators, your most valuable alliance.

Who are these collaborators or partners in your prospect buying decision? Suppliers. Outside vendors. Other clients. Professional service firms. Lawyers. Accountants. Financial advisors. Consultants. Estate planners. Insurance agents. Fund managers. Family. Friends. The list is deep and wide, like a hub and spoke system, connecting together the influences and dispersing the weight across a single decision. It is the original social networking phenomenon, before Facebook or Twitter, and still powers the engine of business today.

My eyes opened to the importance of the collaborator, also known as advisor or center of influence, when I read the bestselling book by Malcolm Gladwell, *The Tipping Point*. He refers to influential people as "mavens," people who possess information and knowledge on a product or subject. The word maven is Yiddish, and it means one who accumulates knowledge.

We all know a Maven—a person who knows all the great deals and everything about a product or service. She reads *Consumer Reports*, and surfs the best-ranked Internet sites to build her case before any purchase. Mavens keep the marketplace honest. Mavens believe knowledge is power and will do what it takes to gather it.

Gladwell explains with this example: "Sometimes when a supermarket wants to increase sales of a given product, they'll put a promotion sticker in front of it, saying something like 'Everyday Low Price!' The price will stay the same. The product will just be featured more prominently. When they do that, supermarkets find that invariably the sales of the product will go through the roof, the same way they would if the product had actually been put on sale." Until a Maven comes along and cries foul, that something is amiss, and forces change.

After reading Gladwell's book, the light bulb went on. In financial services, we deal with highly complex subjects that demand a good deal of time to understand on our own account. No wonder many potential clients are cautious or skeptical about our products and services.

REACH OUT

As I reviewed the buying process for my own products and services, I became increasingly aware that prospects would consult with their outside accounting and legal firms, even their actuaries. These people are my Mavens, requiring a special strategy in the decision making process. At a minimum, I am proactive. I reach out to my Mavens to let them know who we are and how we can add to their knowledge. Often, they believe they already know the subject (although they often do not). Indeed, there is a delicate balance to dispensing knowledge without talking down to a person, and your skill in this regard can pay handsomely.

If you work your Mavens (collaborators) with respect, sincerity and expert, value-added knowledge, your process will generate referrals, shorten the sales cycle, and add to your firm's brand esteem. Consider the impact of this conversation: Ask your prospect, "Who is your outside legal counsel?" He shares, "Jones, Jones and Harrison. Are you working with Fred Smith, its expert in this area?" You flash an understated grin. "He knows our firm well." A defining moment.

To strengthen your collaborator communication strategy, I suggest you read *The Referral of a Lifetime* by Tim Templeton. I guarantee that this book offers the best 132 pages ever written on the subject. I have developed a solid list of collaborators for which I've created a branding, communication and educational strategy. In this way, I am well positioned in their eyes as an expert in my space. I'll discuss this strategy later in Chapter 7, on marketing communications. As you complete your collaborator analysis, the next and final consideration is context.

5. Analysis of Context

The circumstances or context surrounding an idea, conversation or situation shape what is possible, and those possibilities are always changing. Context is often subtle, not easily seen or understood at first glance. Context is also quite subjective. Everyone sizes it up differently.

In building your business and marketing strategy, you need see beyond the obvious, anticipate and remain focused on changes in the market that can enhance your value proposition to your clients. The great Wayne Gretzky sees context as a moving target, and you must stay out in front of it to differentiate your offering; he urges players to skate to where the puck will be, not where it is now. Tax laws and political policies are moving pucks in the financial and professional services arena that constantly shape context.

FIND THE PUCK

Another good example of skating to where the puck will be is to watch changes in how products and services are marketed, and how the distribution channels are organized. The Internet disrupted and upended distribution and communication systems that businesspeople had taken for granted for generations, changing how clients now purchase complex products. While the Internet did not replace direct sales of automobiles, it radically changed consumer behavior before the first showroom visit. They did their homework. They became well-informed buyers who saw value differentiation early on in the sales cycle. It is a whole lot more gratifying to show your value-added to an educated buyer.

Using change to advantage, my firm embraced technology early and developed a strategy to educate our prospects. We benchmarked products and services and quickly understood what could work for us or what would not in the context of our culture. To satisfy the hunger of Internet knowledge-seekers, we built an online knowledge center full of informative content to assist clients and prospects in their educational process. In this context, data and information converts to knowledge and value for clients, and we can change it often to stay responsive, which is crucial to financial and professional services. For example, value in the mutual fund business was once defined by diversification and returns. Nowadays, transparency of fees and services is what the client cares about.

YOUR MARKETING MIX—THE 4 Ps

Now that we have moved through the 5 Cs, it may be helpful to go back to basics to work out more strategy details to influence the buyer. Marketing to prospects by problem solving is different and more difficult than simply promoting a great product or service. There is a key layer of thinking to be done between your marketing analysis (the 5Cs) and your marketing mix (the 4Ps); that is, creating your value through segmentation and targeting, and positioning your services, the essence of strategy. See Chart 6 below.

CHART 6
MARKETING ANALYSIS – THE FIVE Cs

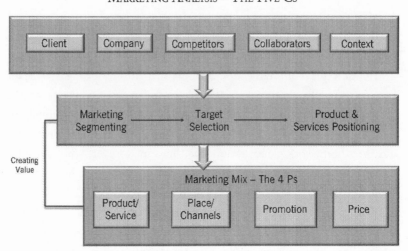

To continue to move forward, consider the classic definition by Harvard Business School Professor Neil Borden. He refers to the "marketing mix" or the 4 Ps: Product, Place, Promotion and Price. With Professor Borden's mix as the foundation, many people have expanded their thinking to encompass the 8 Ps [Chart 7].

I like this concept, as it builds a framework for managing your marketing strategy and activities, however, to succeed with your marketing strategy, remember you need to consider your firm's goals and then focus on your client's needs first. Only when you understand the client's needs should you begin to create a marketing strategy to reach them around the 4 or 8Ps.

I have developed my own 8Ps that I believe balance out the overall strategy for financial and professional services organizations. To the 4 Ps I have added are Perception, Position, Process and Planning. Let's first review Professor Borden's 4P marketing mix.

CHART 7
MARKETING MIX – THE FOUR PS

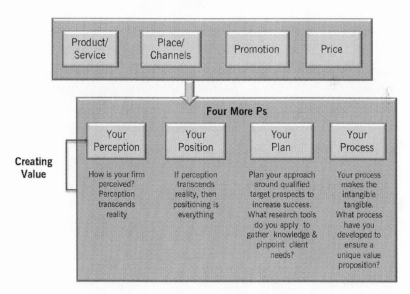

Your Product

When businesspeople talk product, they narrowcast the product as a thing in and of itself, a standalone. That approach is a big mistake. The product is the total package of benefits obtained by the client. It is the value delivered to the client; it is what the client sees as value. Your firm can deliver that value in many complementary ways and even simultaneously: the brand; firm reputation; pre-sales education by salespeople; your process, customer services, post-sales technical support; client references. Understanding all that your product conveys, the value you bring is key to zeroing in on a point of competitive differentiation.

In professional and financial services, we sell ideas, solutions and value propositions, not insurance, not mutual funds, not wills or trusts. Successful salespeople look for ways to find and improve the outcomes their clients seek, and they apply a process to reach the client's desired outcome. The product is the vehicle for you to deliver this desired outcome, or your value proposition.

Your Place

Put simply, place is the network or channel through which your firm distributes its products and services. Place may be a retail kiosk, a big box store, a regional sales force, brokers or agents, or distributor-dealer network. To determine your right approach, begin by first identifying the client's requirements in each phase of the buying process; that is, their buying value chain. Ultimately, you must decide to go direct, use indirect channels or a combination of the two.

- **Direct:** Client meets and deals only with your people directly;
- **Indirect:** A third party under an agreement represents you to the client;
- **Combined:** Sell direct in key regions; use independent contractors in others.

Going direct is a costly affair. You need boots on the ground, a dedicated staff and the ability to shoulder a lot of overhead in back-office support systems. Thus, the economics required to reach primary and secondary segments may be unworkable. If you go indirect or a combination, you must be obsessively selective. Your firm's reputation can hinge, in large part, on who carries your business cards.

No matter how impressive the skill set, every salesperson (direct or indirect) must be carefully trained in your culture, speak from the same playbook, and communicate for clarity, so that the prospect truly understands differentiation.

Your Promotion

The next element of the marketing mix is promotion. In short, how do you get the word out to raise awareness about your offer? Your go-to market strategy requires an integrated marketing communications plan that combines inbound and outbound marketing actions with professional selling efforts. Those marketing actions should include both traditional and digital methods and, ideally, combine the most effective techniques in marketing, communication, public relations, advertising, direct response and social media. I will share with you later some concepts that will help to position you in the market.

Public relations is an effective tool for professional and financial services firms because it allows you to craft a message and communicate it through third parties for greater credibility and, ostensibly, trust. Newsworthy press releases; topical newsletters; well-written and placed articles; informative webcasts and seminars; speeches at industry events, and radio and TV appearances can serve admirably as your brand communication platform. Your goal should not be to sell your services. Instead, let prospects self-discover your firm, message and product.

Public relations, when done with integrity and respect, is a powerful influence-building tool to shape public opinion. But it must not be viewed as commercial hype. It must dispense worthwhile information through well-trafficked communication channels. Its end goal is to inform, inspire and add to the audience's knowledge bank. Effective PR encourages the prospect to act in your favor.

Build and follow a consistent plan for your promotion phase. In my organization, we accomplished the following objectives with good results:

1. Stage a monthly webcast on a topic of interest, hosted by our consultants, or an outside expert as an invited guest. Highly

successful, these webcasts attract 200-300 companies and advisors each month. We recorded and posted them on our website to extend the message to new visitors.

2. Write and distribute one press release monthly to the trade media. Subjects range from new product offerings and staff announcements to new board members or the results of a recent survey. Releases were uploaded to the website to build a news archive.

3. Distribute our own quarterly online corporate magazine to our database of prospects, clients, client advisors, a database which we built organically over time. We drafted in-depth articles on timely topics and use an outside editor to polish. I have learned it is not what you write; it is how you write it.

4. Repurpose each article for distribution to industry magazines, national journals and newspapers. The number of media channels has exploded in recent years and all outlets are on the lookout for fresh and compelling content.

5. Write and distribute thought leadership papers on topics of industry importance. Recently, we investigated how law firms prepare for partner retirement. The distributed results of that study raise awareness in the field. The key here is not to use the study to sell your products or services, but to aim for the reader to self-discover needs that your resources can address.

Writing well-researched reports and white papers are quite powerful tools. They can position you as an expert and dramatically boost your credibility with the client. Our most successful papers and reports tackle the issues confronting clients in their industries. As they read and begin to associate with your position, they self discover your product and service. Often, the prospect is not looking for your service, yet they value the topic and find a useful solution in an educational, non-threatening format.

6. Speak at industry events once per month. We researched industry forums or events where our message added value, and where our target prospects attended. For example, an effective platform is

the National Association of Corporate Directors or the Financial Executives International chapter meetings.

7. Schedule quarterly client/prospect appreciation events. We were privileged to have on our board and as a shareholder Dr. Arthur Laffer, famed economist and advisor to President Reagan. We hosted private dinners for 10 to 15 key prospects to meet Dr. Laffer. The evening brings like-minded people together in a stimulating and non-intrusive environment. While you may not have a Dr. Laffer on your board, you can tap into your local universities for expert authorities. Golf outings at private clubs are also great venues for client/prospect appreciation. Remember, no overt promotion. Build subtle awareness of who you are and what you can do through active listening and casual conversation. Then follow-up with good research.

Your Price

The art of pricing for financial services is far more difficult than for consumer goods and industrial products. Most clients see financial and professional services as intangibles. They don't think about the tangible documents, vehicles or arrangements behind the advice. They concentrate on the outcomes they hope to achieve through your advice, and so often the desired outcomes will take years to evolve and mature.

We sell our time and financial products on a fee-based and/or commission scale. Where do you make your margins, and how do you price for your value-added? If you sell financial planning services, do profits come from your fees or from commissions on the products? Do clients care how you are paid or by whom? Remember, you do not want to sell on price.

What's more, clients typically place different values on a given product or service. Your firm may wish to consider whether to capitalize on these value variations by charging tiered prices to different subsets of clients. The caveat: legal constraints and insurance or securities laws may make this unfeasible. For law firms or accounting firms, consider value billing or success-based fees and incentives, and always speak of fees in terms of value. What separates you from your competitor is not simply that you each do quality work, but that you provide a unique understanding of the value this service provides your client. Hourly billing can be the antithesis of value-based services.

There are two main factors when pricing your products and services. The first is the objective value the product or service delivers to the client. This is the benefit that it provides to your client, even if they don't recognize the benefits you are selling. A client, however, will only pay for their perceived value, which is the second factor. You need to make your value proposition readily apparent to the client, which moves the perceived value closer to the objective value.

One pricing strategy we use to close the gap between objective and perceived value is the fee-based feasibility study. When you deal with a complex sale, you encounter multiple decision makers, all with their own agendas. By charging a small fee for a feasibility study, wherein you evaluate the issue and demonstrate your unique process, you allow decision makers to dip their toes in the water, limit perceived risk and still gain tangible value.

For instance, the human resource director can make a decision to spend $10,000 for a study but he or she will not be authorized to purchase your multi-million-dollar financial product. Lay the groundwork with the study and sell your value-added to all of the decision makers. It is important during your process to focus on the client's issues and show the alternatives and cost of solving his problem. The process brings out the gap and the cost to close it, making your solution value-added. You are pre-conditioning the ultimate sale to the larger body of decision makers.

ADDING 4 MORE PS

As discussed above, Professor Borden set the stage with his 4 Ps. Let's expand your thinking with four more Ps: Perception, Position, Plan and Process.

Your Perception

Perception is a powerful, universal force. It can outweigh physical reality, objective fact, reason, or experience. How we humans perceive our world is our reality. And no matter how precisely or cleverly you create an experience for the prospect, no matter how well you package your solution or market your firm, his brain will translate it into a language, view and experience unique to him. Perception transcends reality. So you must do all you can to put yourself into the brain of your prospect. Observe. Listen. Question. Sense. Engage. Verify.

Although you genuinely believe your firm is the ideal solution, if your prospect doesn't perceive it, you rarely get a second chance to make that first impression.

Your Position

If perception transcends reality, then positioning is everything. Once you select a target market, based on in-depth research, build a compelling and defensible positioning statement which defines your solution, your unique selling proposition, your competitive advantage and how you want to be perceived in the mind of the prospect. Try to do this in 50 words or less, because it forces you to distill your thoughts and discipline your approach.

Some might also call this output your brand statement. Well-defined brands are the supernovas of consulting because they pre-condition and pre-sell. Your brand, whether defined around your firm, solution or process, is at its heart a positive client experience wrapped in a promise to perform. Guard your <u>brand</u> well.

Your Plan

Planning is one of the most important parts of your overall marketing strategy. It begins with your research of your targeted prospect. Knowing as much as you can about your targeted prospect is more important than knowledge of your own products or services. Once you know your buyer inside and out, you can easily start applying your overall marketing strategy.

Your Process

Successful consulting is built on process. Process is your delivery channel for product and services, described in our MERGE collaborative process in the next chapter. Prospects find it difficult to differentiate financial and professional services; they can't hold the product before the sale; they can't experience the service before buying it. Your process makes the intangible tangible. It enables them to understand gaps, explore alternatives, and self-discover your value proposition.

To recap, most prospects decide to buy in five stages. In the first stage, buyers realize they have a need. In most professional and financial service sales, you uncover a value gap to fill that need. Next, buyers recognize they a problem or desire, and begin to search for a solution. They now need to be educated, not sold, on the alternatives. Once educated, and armed with all the information sought, they make their decision, right? Wrong. In the third stage, buyers begin to look at alternatives in detail, and often seek help from trusted advisors—even your competitors.

You can understand then why your process must structure and guide their buying decision, and why it must be objective and evaluate all of the alternatives in a collaborative setting. Finally you need to direct your buyer through implementation and on-going service. In short, build a process that aligns with how your prospect buys, and explain it early and often.

Takeaway

If you search on Amazon for books on marketing, a whopping 376,912 entries appear as of this writing. Anything you want to learn about marketing awaits your one-click buy: marketing management, market strategy, market research, market planning, marketing communications, and the oh-so-friendly *Marketing for Dummies*. My personal favorite is *Marketing Lessons from the Grateful Dead*.

Keep your go-to market strategy simple. Follow the 5 Cs—client, company, competitor, collaborator and context—supported by the 4 Ps, and execute as flawlessly as possible.

4 | THE **MERGE** PROCESS

Success in Consulting

Complex sales require a well-defined collaborative process to clarify client issues, fill in gaps, and identify alternative solutions. When you engage in a collaborative process, you minimize the need to sell, negotiate and close. Keep in mind, people don't like to be sold. But they do like to buy.

Many salespeople attempt to be collaborative consultants. In reality, they are salesmen at heart, pushing the next transaction. And even though selling is the central pulse of business, if you merely push features and benefits, you do not create value for your client.

CONSULTING, NOT SELLING

A genuine consultative approach creates a climate of cooperation to support the client relationship, far preferable to the more brittle mechanics of the typical sales process. True consulting is a pure, systematic and sustainable process that guides your prospect to decide what is in his own best interest, with predictable outcomes to win minds, hearts and budgets.

Whether you earn your living in professional services, business or financial advisory, law or accounting, your process dictates how effectively you solve problems and retain client goodwill. Process-based consulting instills the level of trust needed to turn good prospects into great clients. What's more, a well-defined process buffers you from the need to motivate and persuade reluctant prospects on ideas they may not yet grasp, which can squander precious time.

The more time spent in the consulting process, the less time needed to present and sell solutions. And even though you expend more effort early in the prospect engagement, the collaborative consulting process actually results in a shorter sales cycle. You understand client issues up front and move forward logically and naturally to the sale.

MERGE Ahead

I developed the MERGE Process (**M**agnify. **E**xplore. **R**ecommend. **G**enerate. **E**ngage) to demystify the complex sale for my consultants [Chart 8].

CHART 8
MERGE PROCESS

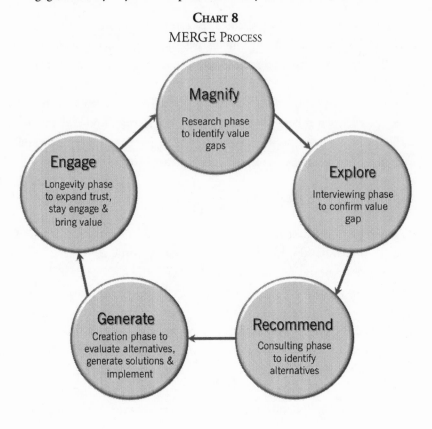

Magnify
Research phase
to identify value
gaps

Explore
Interviewing phase
to confirm value
gap

Recommend
Consulting phase
to identify
alternatives

Generate
Creation phase to
evaluate alternatives,
generate solutions &
implement

Engage
Longevity phase
to expand trust,
stay engage &
bring value

Typically, a complex sale involves multiple decision makers who seek a common resolution for goals and outcomes often in conflict. Because these situations can stubbornly defy any first round of attempts at resolution, prospects reach out to external experts to quarterback the play.

CHANGE IS PAIN

The obvious challenge in a complex sale is that it usually requires change. While change is universally difficult for individuals, it can trigger absolute inertia in many companies. Change carries risk of the unknown, the unfamiliar. We don't like uncertainty or ambiguity. We need to know what lies ahead.

Whenever an organization embarks on a change in status quo, management and staff--whole departments--experience vulnerability. Whether it is true, or only perceived as true, is beside the point. The immediate reaction is resistance. However, if your prospect objectively recognizes that a problem exists, or if he is dissatisfied with his current vendor or situation, he may be inclined to risk change. If he is satisfied or simply can't "see" a problem, he won't.

A thoughtful investment of time and effort in a due diligence process is an essential first step to reduce risk and resistance to change. The way you initiate your process, and the level at which you enter the relationship, will set the length of sales cycles and the ultimate outcome.

The MERGE Process is a simple blueprint to help you guide prospects through a complex decision by lining up all points of interaction in a linear flow, from your research and discovery questions all the way through solution recommendation and final decision. And each collaborative step brings the prospective client closer to the value sought in your solution. The first step in the MERGE Process is research, which we cover in detail in the next chapter.

LOOK AND LEARN

When studying a company for the first time, learn how it makes decisions, who is involved, and at what point. Ironically, most companies don't understand their own decision making process, let alone their long-term implications. Look ahead to consider all possible ramifications of your solution. Recognize, too, that your prospect may know who has final approval authority, but not how that approval is reached. You can assist them with this essential step.

Our MERGE Process parses decisions into bite-sized, easily digestible pieces so that the decision on a major purchase is more naturally appealing to the prospect. You will work rapidly and cleanly toward a mutual objective, identifying the problem and uncovering the best possible solution. And in the process, you will continually qualify the prospect. Typically, the initial contact at the prospect company is the one who influences who you meet, what you speak about, and how quickly issues are uncovered. Never lose sight of your goal: to gain acceptance of your value proposition.

10–5–3–1 FORMULA

My team and I developed a simple way to qualify: the 10–5–3–1 formula [Chart 9]. If you do your research and zero in on ten pre-qualified prospects, then book an initial meeting (at the right level) to propose working through your process, five will take an engagement letter from you. Out of the five, you are likely to be retained by three. Of those three, one will see and accept the benefit of your product or service solution. Don't mistake this for a numbers game and jam through the process. You must do your homework and prepare meticulously for initial meetings with the original ten.

Once you have profiled the prospect with solid research, make contact and secure the actual face-to-face appointment. At this juncture, the courageous quickly break ranks with the timid. It's a funny thing about humans. No one willingly seeks out rejection. But it is well documented that top performers thrive on "no" because it puts them closer to success. I'll admit, I try to minimize rejection by finding a way to meet the right people face-to-face and under favorable conditions.

CHART 9
10 – 5 – 3 – 1 FORMULA

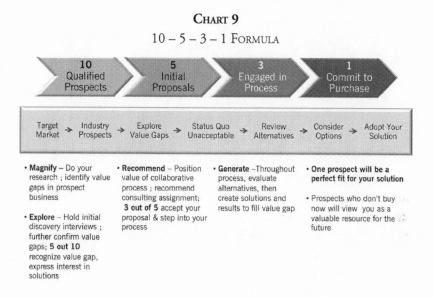

10 Qualified Prospects	5 Initial Proposals	3 Engaged in Process	1 Commit to Purchase

Target Market →	Industry Prospects →	Explore Value Gaps →	Status Quo Unacceptable →	Review Alternatives →	Consider Options →	Adopt Your Solution

- **Magnify** – Do your research ; identify value gaps in prospect business
- **Explore** – Hold initial discovery interviews ; further confirm value gaps; **5 out 10** recognize value gap, express interest in solutions

- **Recommend** – Position value of collaborative process ; recommend consulting assignment; **3 out of 5** accept your proposal & step into your process

- **Generate** –Throughout process, evaluate alternatives, then create solutions and results to fill value gap

- **One prospect will be a perfect fit for your solution**
- Prospects who don't buy now will view you as a valuable resource for the future

When most salespeople search out new clients, they mistakenly enter the discussion at too low a level in the organization, or allow a higher-level decision maker to push them down the ladder. When this happens, the prospect has already determined the need and solution he wants. Often, I encounter this situation when human resource (HR) contacts think they know what I am selling and attempt to lead the conversation to existing programs and vendor selection, then a request-for-proposal (RFP) process.

This situation can be exacerbated by the CEO, even after you have a top line discussion. She may send you down to HR, and characterize the discussion in simple product and service terms. Either way, you've lost control. Later, we'll discuss how you can avoid this dilemma.

MOVE IT UP

If stopped at the HR level, it usually involves an RFP, which only means they are focused on product and price. Unless you identified the value gap and helped create the specifications for the RFP, you are reduced to one of dozens blindly responding to an exercise that often leads nowhere. Better to do your research and enter the company at a much higher level with the goal of discussing key initiatives. So how do you meet the right people under favorable conditions? You have done your research and identified key initiatives:

- You have a good sense of need, means and motive
- You have attracted a collaborator or referral by another respected person
- You know the identities of key decision makers, influencers and how they relate
- Who you are is already recognized because of your strategic marketing
- Everyone on the prospect team is committed to the meeting

In Step 2 of the MERGE Process, you need to "explore." Take your research and develop a plan of action with well-thought-out questions about the prospect's situation. Questioning is an important part of the process; it sets you apart as a collaborative consultant. We will discuss the details of effective questioning later in this chapter.

No Cold Calls

Only a limited number of companies are in the market for your products and services; however, many more have need and, if carefully identified, would have an interest in your offer. Of course, the odds are also high that your prospect already owns or uses some version of your product or service and has no perceived need for your value proposition.

Remember from the introduction, the incumbent vendor is in the key position. Most companies are not going to rip up the sidewalk to make a change away from your competitor unless the reason is extremely compelling. That's why I find a more educational-based approach—one that presents informative market data (not product data)—persuades the prospect to agree to a personal meeting. For example, if you can credibly present market data that indicates your prospect's top competitor is growing market share by ten-percent-per-year, while his is flat, he is going to pay attention to your value proposition.

Avoid cold calling as an initial call. Strive for room temperature contact through referrals, white papers, network meetings--some touchpoint to spark familiarity. Today, we are fortunate. Presence on the Internet, online marketing and social media help to transform prospects into self-discoverers and self-qualifiers. We Google and click on landing pages to investigate what interests us, letting that interest pull us into a conversation.

There is nothing wrong with cold calling; it is the lifeblood of many sales practices. But why pick the neighbor's front door lock when you can be invited in as a guest? Warm calling is the hallmark of a successful consultant. Put simply, leverage your marketing efforts (more later) so that your prospect reaches out to you with interest. White papers, speaking engagements, and webinars are all ways to redirect prospects toward you.

THE INITIAL CALL

With the first phone contact, your only objective is to schedule the meeting. Introduce yourself briefly, make a short statement or two about your initial research or the data they requested and your process, and then set up the face-to-face meeting. Offer market data or something of value, and this call will unfold naturally.

Refrain from long discussions. Often, after some email exchange where the prospect agrees to meet, my assistant calls the assistant at the prospect company and schedules the meeting time. If you are fortunate to have a finder, collaborator or influencer involved, ask him to arrange the meeting. He can break the ice, set you up as an expert, and lay the groundwork for trust in the process.

I also like to forward our corporate profile in advance of the meeting to avoid lost time in an initial meeting engaged in show and tell. Many times it is more effective to send along a research report, authored by us, on relevant industry issues, rather than a corporate brochure. We will discuss these tools later and their major impact on setting you up as an expert.

This time is prime time to learn about them. Your selling process must be about your client, not about you. Prospects can gather all of the information they need online, or read materials you send in advance of the meeting.

PRE-MEETING CALL

I credit part of step two in the MERGE Process to Tom Hummer, a savvy stock broker from San Diego who occasionally collaborated with me on client engagements. Tom was a real pro at asking probing questions that pulled the right information from the prospect. Prior to the meeting, we would schedule a pre-call. Here's how it works. Let's say a meeting is scheduled for next Wednesday with the CFO of a target company. We arrange a 30-minute conference call to set the agenda for the face-time meeting; we gather additional information; and we gauge who else will attend the meeting. This pre-call pays major dividends. Simply say to the prospect, "I would like to have a call prior to the meeting to confirm some information I gathered, so we can make our meeting next week more productive." If you're working with a finder like Tom, the pre-call rolls out like the red carpet on Oscar night.

Whatever you do, be careful not to talk too much. And don't try to sell anything. The success key is to gather and confirm information from your research to make the meeting more productive. I learn a lot in these pre-calls. And they seem to create a buzz in the organization. When I arrive at the face-meeting, I'm always pleased to see how many other prospect members join the meeting.

Here is an example of a pre-call: One of my collaborators sets up a meeting with his client to discuss a supplemental executive retirement plan (SERP). He mentioned the company was looking into this as a vehicle to help attract and retain some key people. Whenever I hear a product or concept mentioned, my objective is to circle back to the original issue the product is intended to solve the value gap. It is a natural for you to begin answering questions about a SERP but if you do, you are no different from the other product-oriented salespeople. Someone planted the idea. Now, your goal is to initiate questioning of company objectives, internal processes and expected outcomes.

So my collaborator set up a call with the CFO and went through his normal introduction. Once he turned the call over to me, I began to probe with a few key questions. *"It is my understanding that you are interested in adopting a SERP? What issues will the SERP solve for you?"*

CFO:	"We have a stock option plan that is underwater and we need something to help attract and retain some key people."
WMD:	"Have you looked at other alternatives?"
CFO:	"Yes, we are also looking at a nonqualified deferred compensation plan."
WMD:	"Which one do you see as the best alternative at this point, or are you still analyzing this?"
CFO:	"We like the benefits of the SERP, but as a company we like the cost and accounting treatment of a deferred compensation plan."
WMD:	"What would be three outcomes you would like to see in the ideal plan?"
CFO:	"That is a good question; let's see . . . I guess we would like to see the benefit tied to the performance of the company, since we will be replacing this with stock. Second, we would like some kind of vesting to tie the person to the company and, finally, keep the company's cost down."

At this point, based on all of this information, I have a clearer idea of how to design a solution for the company. But this call is not the time to offer a solution. My objective was to gather additional information. Now I will continue with more research on what others have done, write up more questions, and prepare to float these questions to the CFO and his group. I simply thank him for his insight, determine if there is any more information he thinks I should have, and then prepare for the face-meeting.

The deeper level of research you do, and the more additional information you gain in the pre-call, the better you can identify the major issues, initiatives and goals in play within the prospect organization. This research allows you to learn and speak the prospect language, as well as frame the conversation on its priorities. Research is so important that I dedicated an entire chapter to it and provided you with a host of tools. Knowledge builds trust as you walk into the first face-to-face meeting.

THE FACE-TO-FACE MEETING

On the day of the personal meeting, arrive early with eye-in-the-sky vision. Enter the lobby. Observe everything: signage, visitors, energy levels, the mission or values statement on the wall. When you sign in, scan the sheet and notice if any competitors, key vendors or one of your collaborators might be scheduled with the prospect that day.

Remember, you have barely five seconds to make a visual impression, so stand (do not sit) in the prospect's office lobby. Look sharp and ready to greet your contact. Don't force her to look down on you slunk in that Corbusier chair. Stand tall, confident and professional. Small touches deliver big impact. I know this is basic selling 101, but we all should remember what a difference this makes.

Personal meetings are ideal for collecting history on the prospect's past successes, current activity and future goals. Find the gaps. Work the gaps together to identify issues and discuss possible solutions. Interview the prospect and verify information already gathered, and gather more. Sell nothing, no product or service, even if you feel the door is open. Focus only on the consulting process you plan to recommend.

If the prospect brings up my products and services, I might say, "I am not sure if there is a fit yet. I need to understand your objectives and gather some additional information." Pardon the cliché but prospects don't care how much you know until they know how much you care. Stay focused on understanding their situation and probe for solvable issues by resisting the temptation to sell.

Do your best to control the structure of this initial meeting. Begin with the polite business card exchange, verify the topic and confirm the time set aside. I might say something like, "Based on our phone conversation last week, I understand the purpose of the meeting is to discuss options for helping the company attract and retain its key people." Look for verification.

"I also understand that we have one hour, is that correct?" This gives you an opportunity to organize your materials and to set people at ease. Leave 15 minutes at the end to make sure you can get questions answered. Even more important than structure is your skill at guiding the prospect through a well-thought-out interviewing process. Having an agenda ready demonstrates organized thinking and helps the prospect focus on the flow of your topics.

My goal at this meeting is to establish credibility, gather information and describe our consulting process (Step three of the MERGE Process) and how we work. I also want to build rapport, so I use people's first names and actively listen to concerns. Believe me, attention to this detail makes a difference.

Personalize the meeting by making referential statements: "Mary, this is one of the issues you brought up on the phone call." Use the art of storytelling to help them see, hear and sense possible solutions: "We had a client recently who faced a similar situation . . ." Again, pardon the cliché, but this is classic Feel/Felt/Found strategy: We feel your pain points; we felt the same way when our client faced this situation, and this is what we found out. It's all about association. It can only be accomplished by good questions and good listening.

In those first few minutes of the initial meeting, you must be a consultant and forget about your products and services. Many salespeople do not spend enough time considering the questions that they must ask to position their value proposition. Like John in our introduction, they jump into features and benefits far too soon in the process.

QUESTIONS BEHIND THE QUESTION

The MERGE Process is very different; we begin our "explore" step by asking questions in a well-organized mode. Never begin by asking about product lines or status of current providers. Your prospect will dive into a defensive mode. Ask about the company's key initiatives to open up the collaborative process. Remember, in the pre-call meeting, I did not discuss the product we sell. Effective questioning requires comprehensive research and preparation to maximize the outcome of this meeting, which will lead to an engagement by the prospect to help him with his issues.

From your research, develop your questioning plan. Think through everything you will need to know to fully understand your prospect's issues, so you can start to discuss possible alternatives. Develop the list of questions in advance so you can focus on listening to the prospect's responses instead of trying to think about more questions.

If I understand that the prospect's objective is to attract and retain key people, I open by asking, "What are you doing right now?" I want to fully understand the status quo so I can determine if there is a gap where I can offer value. All my initial questions are focused on verifying information, determining what has transpired so far and what, if anything, the company looks to accomplish. You need to ask open-ended questions that require more than a yes or no answer.

Even if the prospect mentions my product or service as what the company is exploring, I don't go there yet. The company may still be testing you to see if, in fact, you have the characteristics of a trusted advisor.

On one initial call recently, the prospect asked if we funded deferred compensation plans with life insurance products. My response was, "Many of our clients have used life insurance to fund their plans; however, I am not sure it is the right decision for you yet. The beauty of our process, and I'll explain more later, is that we look at all of the alternatives based on your objectives, tax situation, cost of money, and more. Insurance is only one of the alternatives to consider."

BINOCULAR VIEW

Next, I ask questions to better understand the prospect's direction. I am gauging whether his focus is fear, needs or desire. As the discussion turns to the gap, I'm sure he had a good idea of the gap before I arrived. I want to focus on what it is that prevents the company from getting to its intended destination. It is much easier to secure your role as a trusted advisor when you ask the right questions from the outset. Equally important, frame your questions to reflect the concerns of each level in the organization involved in decision making.

Use prepared questions from your research to ask solid questions that illustrate your understanding of the prospect's changing industry dynamics. Focus on his industry and its key challenges. Prospective clients don't want to talk with people selling products or services. They are always on the lookout for industry insight that can help them avoid risks and capture opportunities. Your research can help you deliver value by using industry benchmarks and information to contribute to more informed decisions and enable prospects to meet goals and objectives.

Let me give you an example of questions from my research. I had an opportunity to meet with the CFO and director of human resources for a large hospital group. The group was a major player and ran more than 50 hospitals. My research told me that there were 6,500 hospitals with combined annual revenue of about $700 billion. The top fifty organizations (my prospect was one) were responsible for 30 percent of industry revenue, indicating fragmentation.

I also discovered through research that demand for hospital services is driven by demographics and advances in medical care and technology. The profitability of individual companies depends on "efficient operations." Hospitals also compete for physicians, and seek to attract desirable doctors with state-of-the-art equipment, and an attractive work environment. Although the majority of hospital employees earn low to modest pay, the high income of doctors and other specialist contribute to higher overall earnings. My research also showed that there is a shortage of doctors in the marketplace, somewhere between 50,000 and 130,000. Further, there is a lot of consolidation and firms buying up physician practices.

My research pointed to a recent study by S&P Rating Services that during the past two to three years pension costs have risen at double-digit rates for hospitals with defined benefit programs. Although hospitals certainly treat patients, their largest clients are managed-care companies. When I examined my prospect's business profile, I found all these risk factors applicable, none of which I would have known without the research effort.

Based on my research, the following four questions emerged and created a binocular field of view on the main issues:

1. *How was the hospital dealing with the shortage of physicians in the marketplace?*

2. *What programs, if any, was the hospital using to attract and retain physicians?*

3. *What issues arose with these programs? Did the hospital have any data on what others were doing in the field?*

4. *Had the hospital calculated costs to attract and retain a physician?*

As I did, you will discover that the questioning process is designed to stimulate discussion and pinpoint the issues. Then you can get more specific. For example, I asked, "Please describe the three outcomes you wish to bring about as a result of designing a program for your physicians? And the hospital team came up with three. Your prospect will as well.

Recently, in responding to an RFP, I asked the CFO of the company the last question. He said price, quality of service and web experience of his participants in the deferred compensation plan. When I further questioned him, he referred to price as cost to the company. Then I asked him to define cost to the company and he said, "The impact on the company's profit and loss statement." Had I assumed price meant fees I would have lowered mine or been defensive. Questioning helps you determine the outcome they want and it keeps the process collaborative.

From your research, list questions you would like to bring to that first meeting. Remember, the first meeting objective is to understand their situation and determine the gap. It is not to sell your products or services. Don't even bring it up. At this stage, the prospect or I normally ask, "What is the next step?" At this point we discuss and recommend (Step 3 of our MERGE Process) and ask if it is appropriate to send an engagement letter.

We explain that the engagement letter will outline the process and how we work. Get the prospect's input on the process and steps. Clients want to buy according to their own process. Clients want to be part of a collaborative process to determine the solutions, which is why I design the engagement letter around how they want to buy. I might outline my thoughts on each step, then get their buy in. Many times I suggest sending a draft of the engagement letter to provide an opportunity for client input on objectives and the process, which adds more involvement and further encourages buy-in.

A Way In

One way to walk away from a face-to-face meeting with concrete results (even though you're not selling) is to recommend ("R" in the MERGE Process) a reasonably priced feasibility study or consulting engagement that tackles a specific issue. This strategy is also a qualifier. If the prospect team cannot agree to solve a smaller issue and pay a nominal fee to do so, it will not ultimately spend hundreds of thousands on your consulting products or services. You'll find a copy of a sample engagement letter in the Appendix.

Remember, your major goal and only sale in the initial meeting is to gather information and come to agreement on the gap, and to sell your capabilities and the consulting process you use. When the client does not recognize the gap in the first meeting, do not follow up by sending or recommending an engagement letter. You must first establish the gap and get buy-in that they are looking for solutions to close it. That gap must also be quantifiable so you can show your impact. You may have to spend more time in Step 2; don't rush the consulting process, or you'll be recommending a solution to a problem they do not perceive.

SELLING YOUR PROCESS

A number of years ago, one of my board members told me a story that hit home. It is a good example of how to set up a well-thought-out process with good research and knowledge of your prospect's business. It is also a good illustration of how to sell your process by providing value-added around the issues you uncover. He was the CEO of a major food company that decided at the board level to hire a strategic planning company to handle a market repositioning. One board member suggested a major, well-known firm; another member a second firm; more recommendations came from other members. A beauty contest ensued.

Three out of four firms came in during the initial face-to-face meeting armed with heavy credentials, client testimonials, and the how-great-we-are yadda-yadda presentation. The fourth firm, a virtual unknown, was recommended by a lone board member.

The unknown firm built a well-researched case study on the food company and its industry. That first face-to-face meeting was a brilliant exercise in Socratic logic, with the contestant asking intelligent questions, actively listening and gathering seemingly obscure information.

At the next meeting, the fourth firm began with, "Based on our pre-vious meeting and our own research, we now understand your industry, and believe your problem is logistics and the locations of your warehouses." They went on to discuss the issue, got buy-in from the board to further verify their assessment, and said, "If selected, we will approach this assignment with sharp focus on these two issues and these possible solu-tions." The firm then estimated cost savings, specified value to be gained by their step-by-step process, and discussed how they could improve the company's profits.

No canned presentation. Only original research, critical thinking and problem-solving structure, delivered in a collaborative way. This clever, lesser-known firm found a way to speak informally (between meetings) with several executives in the food company for added input on its draft proposal prior to the second meeting. In this way, the presentation team hit close to the board's target on topics of interest. In short, firm four spent a lot of time collaborating with people who had skin in the game and wanted to be part of the ultimate solution and show how it could bring value.

The board brought firm four back to the final meeting for the good news and bad news. The good news: Everyone was impressed with its approach, knowledge of the business, and understanding of the issues. The bad news: The board preferred to first hire the firm on a smaller project with one of its subsidiaries. After all, its members really didn't know the firm as well as its competition.

To its credit, firm four passed on the project. Its lead presenter explained, "We both know what the issues are with your parent company, and if we're hired at the subsidiary level, we can't bring you the value. We'll pass on this assignment, but we are flattered that you chose us." The board sent the feisty group to the lobby for a quick break, and then brought them back in. And hired them.

THE **MERGE** FIVE-STEP PROCESS

The MERGE Process is powerfully simple, evolving over five integrated steps. Whether your firm specializes in estate and financial planning, accounting, law, real estate or employee benefits, you need to develop the key components of a process-driven approach, unique to your capabilities. A simple step approach: [Chart 10]

M*agnify* your understanding of client issues. Use research to formulate thoughtful questions. Discover needs. Begin to diagnose the situation. Be guided by a collaborative discussion.

E*xplore* alternatives for solving prospect problems. Draw outlines for optimal solutions. Refer and discuss. Zero in on alternatives and focus on presenting your value proposition.

R*ecommend* your consulting process as a way of analyzing alternatives. Establish framework and time frame. Gain agreement to the steps in your process. Confirm the engagement.

G*enerate* project specifications through your consulting process, assemble your team, build the work product and focus on being engaged. Review alternatives for your client's issues.

E*ngage* throughout entire process. Stay fully connected to the client. Scan for opportunities to problem solve, and produce results with your value proposition.

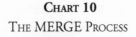

CHART 10
THE MERGE PROCESS

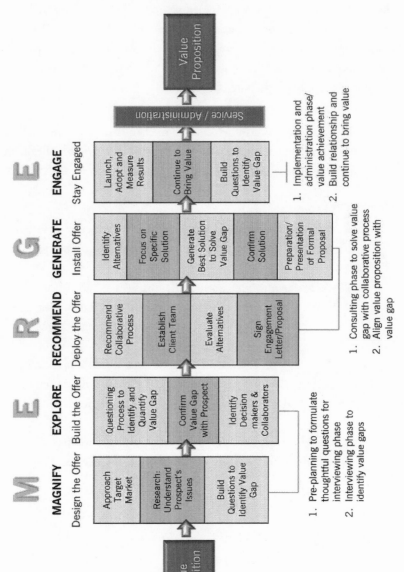

A WORD ON TEAMING

Once your client has agreed to engage you, you need to identify your client team and establish the closing or implementation date. A simple, realistic timetable sets everyone's expectations and, importantly, keeps the process moving forward and paves the way for a series of small and manageable decisions to occur [sample in Appendix]. This gives you more control of the sales cycle.

Begin with the end in mind. You ask, "If our process is successful and you implement our recommendations, when do you expect the new program to begin?" A date is given. Ask, "Do we need board approval?" If so, your next statement: "With a January 1 start date, you will need to conduct enrollment in December, so we might want to pencil in an October or November board meeting. What do you think? And who would approve recommendations prior to the board meeting, so we have time to prepare?"

An important step during the recommend phase of the process is to help the prospect determine his best team members. You have a lot of experience with the topic, so suggest key members from legal, accounting, human resources--those who will be impacted. Perhaps there are outside advisors who should be included on the team. In this way, you manage the buying processes, keep surprises at bay, and interact with all of the decision makers. Be on the lookout for these key members on the prospect's team as you enter the first two steps of the MERGE Process.

While these steps may seem painfully obvious to you, it is truly amazing how many salespeople trip up at this stage and lose momentum.

Step 1—Magnify Your Understanding

In Step 1, you find your inner Socrates. Prepare your open-ended questions to discuss in Step 2, as we discussed earlier. Take out your magnifying glass and look deep into your research. Find the information to prepare you for that initial meeting and to increase your chances of being invited back to a second meeting. By preparing with your questioning plan from your research, you identify the most valuable information. I will demonstrate in our Go-to-Market Strategy that getting in the door isn't the hard part; it is staying in that gets you the results you want.

Sophisticated buyers, especially those at large companies, have all heard from the top sales and consulting professionals in your field. They have also engaged many experts over the years. You must make a favorable impression with your knowledge and understanding of their business, industry and key issues to be invited back for Step 2.

In fact, according to a 2010 study by CSO Insight, 53 percent of sales organizations report that less than half of their first meetings result in a second meeting. You only get one shot at making a good first impression. Research and preparation are key. "Preparing for the Initial Contact—The Research Mindset" chapter gives you the tools needed to make that strong first impression. Don't take this lightly. It is crucial to getting the MERGE Process off to a good start.

Step 2—Explore the Alternatives

This step is your first contact face to face with the company, and you now have your foot in the door. It is designed to explore, not to sell anything.

Remember how the meeting was set up on your initial contact, and your prospect's initial interest. Begin the meeting with the topic that got you in the door, discuss industry issues, then gently probe pain points. Ask more questions from your research. In the initial part of the meeting, based on your research, it is best to assume the prospect has similar issues, needs and concerns as others in its industry. As you continue to explore with questions and listening, you will fine-tune the focus. Begin to formulate your best diagnosis of the primary and secondary issues facing your prospect.

This is a self-discovery step for both you and your client. Intelligent questioning helps the client to focus on her issues and gaps in the current situation, while you learn more. This step digs deeper to help define the extent and financial impact of prospect problems. The process is designed to bring out the client's dissatisfaction with the status quo and help to define their objectives for providing a solution, even if it is not your product or service. One of the biggest reasons sales are lost is because of a poor understanding of prospect priorities.

Step 2 is the first big step the client makes toward some action; it will be important to follow the process and not jump ahead with solutions to problems not yet fully defined. Let's say your practice specializes in the 401(k) retirement business. You need to probe to find issues with the client's current plan as it impacts key initiatives at the company. You need to build your value proposition to show your capabilities, the impact on the company, and the cost of doing nothing. Then you need to prove it through examples with other clients.

As part of Step 2, you could offer a comparison of the prospect's current plan with best practices or show a peer review drawn from your research. This action demonstrates your investment in research, as well as your objectivity, and also opens up an opportunity to probe with additional questions.

Step 2 sets the stage to launch your engagement process. You and the prospect should have both identified what the issues are and how wide the gap is, and the cost of remaining at status quo. If not, this is the stage to flesh it out. The smaller the gap, the less likely the prospect will take any action. The wider the gap, the greater the desire to take immediate action to solve his issues—and close the gap.

Do not bring solutions to Step 2, only potential alternatives, even if you think the solution is obvious. Store your alternatives for later in the consulting process, and discuss the details once you have been engaged. Your review is designed to identify gaps and potential shortfalls in the prospect's thinking, behavior or operational style. Use the opportunity to inform and educate the prospect on key issues. Prioritize the most threatening gaps. If the prospect team doesn't begin to make small but important decisions at this point, stay focused and tuck away the gaps in an action folder for a follow-up meeting.

For instance, let's assume your prospect is interested in engaging you to solve a problem of low participation levels in their 401(k) plan, or to help highly compensated employees offset government restrictions on deferrals. Rather than suggest an alternative such as a company match to the 401(k) to help increase participant levels, keep probing.

Find out how the situation impacts the growth of the company or impacts profits, competitiveness or the retention of key employees. You may know the answer, but now is the time to dig deeper with open-ended questions, such as, "In your view, what impact have the low participation levels in your 401(k) plan had on your competitive position in the market?"

One solution might be to increase the 401(k) match for all employees, and you can share the merits of this later when you discuss the cost of alternative solutions. More analysis may be in order, but at least your prospect is engaged and closer to some level of decision.

A well-organized diagnostic yields all sorts of worthwhile fruit, including which individuals are responsible for which element in the decision making tree. Your prospect views you as credible and a person of influence who can offer objective advice. Again, the process reinforces your value as you identify, evaluate and probe into their issues, uncovering hidden opportunities as you go.

In the explore step, your objective is to guide the prospect team through their current situation to identify priority issues and create understanding on possible solutions. Importantly, lay out all of the solutions, not just your own. Fidelity to the collaborative process demands that we examine all solutions to close the gap and the price tag attached to each.

Hopefully, now team members understand the problems, are invested in the process, and openly discuss potential solutions. Now you can continue to educate how your solution, among others, closes the needs gap, and why your consulting process helps the prospect team select the right alternative.

Many times during this step, it is also helpful to bring in others from your organization destined to play key roles in upcoming steps. This expansion reassures the prospect-client. After all, it is your team who will deliver the long-term services required to maintain the client relationship. I normally do this in the follow-up meeting (still in this step), when we lay out our proposed steps in our consulting process.

During the exploratory step, it is imperative to understand the decision making process associated with each alternative. This dynamic may alter timelines. Keep the engagement on track by adjusting any timelines at this point. And remember that it is essential to manage client expectations during this step, as you explore the alternatives. You are the expert in your field. Continue to educate, inform and offer encouragement to help the client through the decision making process.

By keeping the discussion fresh, fluid and collaborative, you can sell your expertise as a problem solver with knowledge of the prospect situation and possible alternatives. Now you're ready to move forward into Step 3, which is to recommend your consulting process.

Step 3—Recommend the Engagement; Prospect Agrees to the Process

When you return to your office following the meeting, you need to review your notes and begin analyzing the information you've gathered in order to draft your proposed consulting engagement. Make it a point to recommend the steps needed for their team to evaluate the alternatives. Step 3 is a major step in the MERGE Process. You are outlining possible alternatives, suggesting your consulting process, and helping the prospect to determine which direction is best for his situation. Your goal: to secure a commitment to your collaborative consulting process.

During Step 2, we discussed our initial timetable around the desired solution and developed a solid understanding of the decision making process for solutions. In the 401(k) example, going before the plan committee was a key step in the decision process, followed by a presentation to the company's board of directors. We need to build that into our engagement proposal. The letter must outline the issues uncovered, the value proposition, the prospect's objectives, the process you will follow, your team, the timetable and your compensation.

In my experience, if you send a draft for prospect review, she will give you valuable input and begin to buy in as a willing participant in the process. Next, present the final letter in person; personalization strengthens your closing ratio. Think of this step as the small sale before the big one. Your objective is to sell the company on your process and to get commitment to move forward.

As this step evolves, create the framework for your solution and narrow down the alternatives. Begin to focus on the one alternative that carries the greatest value—the one the prospect-client will consider for final review. At this point, it is not uncommon to bring in outside advisors to support your final conclusions.

Using our 401(k) issue again as an example, we vetted all of the alternatives for fixing prospect issues and identified the cost of each. One alternative was to install a separate nonqualified plan to carve the highly compensated out of the 401(k) and treat the problem directly with a separate solution. You are now drilling down into the recommendation in more detail, with a focus on implementing the solution.

Normally, we draft an overview of our findings, with supporting data and facts so decision makers can clearly see we have examined all options and are in a position to recommend the best solution. Now is the time to move into implementation.

Anyone successful in sales or consulting knows the real work begins the day after the sale is made. Our first sale is to get hired for the consulting engagement. Even if you're not charging a fee for this process, it is important to lay out the steps in a formal letter and secure the client commitment signature. How many times have you landed a contract on a verbal handshake, only to have it fall apart before all the paperwork is complete? To help prevent an unraveling of the engagement, start working on Step 4 immediately. Engage now. Maintain client involvement, discussion and interaction at every reasonable juncture.

Step 4—Generate Project Specifications; Get Things Done

You are now at the delivery stage and ready to get things done. Your signed engagement letter maps out your project specifications in full detail. You have outlined your team in your engagement letter. Now it is time to ensure the new client selects appropriate team members on its side to continue the collaborative process.

As we discussed earlier, you also need to map out a timetable of events and deliverables to track and meet expectations. I always begin by asking the anticipated adoption or implementation date and the final approval date. For my business, final approval is the official decision by the board of directors. As I build my timetable for the project, I might ask, "If the effective date for the plan is January 1, and we need to enroll everyone in December, we should look for board approval in October so we can have final documents prepared in November. Does that make sense?" Then we work backwards to fill in the events, the decisions, and people we need to involve each step of the way.

This sequence works like magic and eliminates surprises. Remember, the company hasn't fully bought your solution yet. This step is critical in helping the new client review alternatives and self-discover yours as the best one. Stay focused and follow the process.

At this point, you should have full buy-in from the client's team members. Typically, they will coach you and help prepare materials for the final approval. Everyone has a vested interest now, and the prospect team wants to see the project completed with your recommendations.

If you have followed the MERGE Process, final approval for your value proposition should occur now, flowing automatically through each step of the process, and leading to that all-important final close. As you deepen the relationship using your engagement process, the client commitment grows. Decisions are made; fees are paid.

Step 5—Engage, Engage, Engage

You must keep your new client engaged, focused, and committed to follow-through. I've seen many relationships undone over the years by overconfident salespeople who assumed too much. Relationships are built in small steps, gestures, and conversations. And both parties need to recommit with some frequency, even if in unspoken and understated ways.

Stay engaged at a respectful distance, without annoying the client with too many eager communiqués. As you implement the consulting contract, keep the client informed throughout the process. Communicate milestones and insights. Share timely observations and industry activity.

An occasional email is fine, but don't rely solely on this cold medium. Be different. Send a formal letter. Dash off a handwritten note. Make a phone call. Meet for lunch. I suspect anyone over 35 secretly yearns for a little less Twittering and more old-school communicating.

Again, these suggestions may seem obvious, however, do not underestimate their power to build long-term value and repeat engagements. Your client privately wants reassurance that he has made the right choice in you, your process, and your solution. It is your responsibility to deliver that reassurance in everything you do, from the point of first contact to the close and onward.

5 | PREPARING FOR INITIAL CONTACT

The Research Mindset

"Luck is what happens when preparation meets opportunity," proclaimed the Roman philosopher Seneca in the first century A.D. While this truism has stood the test of time, one wonders if it can withstand the digital revolution of the modern age.

How do you find the time and patience to prepare for meetings amid tides of information? On an average day, the average American consumes 34 gigabytes and 100,000 words of information, according to a 2009 study by the University of California, San Diego. U.S. households consumed approximately 3.6 zettabytes of information in 2008. One zettabyte equals 1,000,000,000 trillion bytes or the same as thick paperback novels stacked seven feet high over the entire United States, the study explains.

Although the term information overload has already become a cliché, it is here to stay. So what does an ambitious salesperson do to prepare for meetings? Develop the research mindset.

If you think and act as a salesperson, you sell products or services. You are transactional. If you think and act as a collaborative consultant, you offer solutions. You problem solve. There is only one direct route to competitive advantage: Build workable solutions around gaps in your prospect's business performance in order to improve his financial performance.

It all begins with research. Would you walk into a showroom and buy a new $350,000 Bentley Brooklands with no questions asked? Would you trust your heart to a cardiovascular surgeon whose credentials you don't know? Extreme examples, yes, but they parallel a salesperson's failure to research a prospect situation with a high-value sale at stake.

KNOW TO GROW

Too many salespeople fly by the seat of their pants in the selling process. They walk into prospect meetings with a limited understanding of the company, its history, the industry, or the CEO's pain points. I talk to many salespeople in my role as CEO of a major company, and it bewilders me why they know so little about our company and our issues. Like me, most business leaders wish you knew more.

Research is one of the most critical actions in the selling process and is central to a successful consulting engagement. And paper-thin preparation is costly. Early in my business, when I experienced research-challenged salespeople, I quickly nipped it by backfilling my own research so I could step into their not-ready-for-prime-time shoes and save the sale. I upped the ante on the whole firm, set new standards and expected more.

Still, in years of sitting in the CEO chair, I've politely extended the requisite 15 minutes to one eager salesperson after another who came to call with mindless enthusiasm. They didn't know me, our company, our goals, our problems, or what we cared about.

In 1998, a focus group of IBM's largest clients revealed that "Reps [salespeople] have inadequate knowledge of our business and our industry." In a Harvard case study titled *The Transformation of IBM*, a major IBM client was quoted: "They [IBM salespeople] knew nothing about our business, nor did they attempt to learn much." Other large IBM clients were asked what they expect from a salesperson: "The number one thing we expect is excellent knowledge of our company, our industry, and the environment in which we do business," citing product knowledge in second place.

Interestingly, these clients did not indicate the need for expert product, engineering or scientific knowledge. Instead, "we only expect the rep to **understand** the product line." A decade later, companies are still saying that their consultants and advisors do not know their business or the issues in their industry.

Here is how one of the greatest generals in the history of the United States regarded the role of research in his success:

"I have studied the enemy all my life.

I have read the memoirs of his generals and leaders.

I have read his philosophers.

I have studied in detail every damned one of his battles.

I know exactly how he will react under any circumstance.

So when the time comes I'm going to whip the hell out of him."

When you consider that General George S. Patton could neither read nor write until the age of twelve, his accomplishments are all the more remarkable.

DATA TO INSIGHT

Research is the body builder of intelligent consulting. And facts are like muscles: You can allow them to waste them away from lack of use or strengthen them with a little effort. Quality research goes beyond assembling facts. Look at research in a linear way. You scan resources to find chunks of raw data. You sift through it, discard the useless and organize the relevant into valuable information, ready for analysis. Only when that information is analyzed with a critical eye does research morph into knowledge, insight and, if you are fortunate, even wisdom.

When you and your team meet for the first time to discuss the challenges of a given prospect, make it your mission to master the following:

- Fully understand the situation from every angle
- Adapt your well-structured process to shape the best solution
- Determine which best practices offer highest probability of results

If you know more about your prospect than the competitor, in effect, you neutralize your competition. Research answers are hidden in plain sight. And you can find them for zero cost. When you do, you'll go directly to the head of the line in the parade of vendors competing for the prospect's business. Ironically, top-performing salespeople sell the least because they know the most about their client.

As few years ago, one of our collaborators, a 401(k) provider, wanted to introduce me to one of his clients. I learned he was trying to position our services as better than the current provider, which is actually the wrong approach. I explained our research process, then asked him to set up the meeting differently and gave him some sound bites from our research.

His healthcare client is one of the largest suppliers of contract nurses in the country. The company's ability to attract and retain a steady flow quality nurses was compromised, posing a serious risk to its future. This fact was clearly outlined in the CEO's letter to the shareholders and the company's 10K filing. My research confirmed a national shortage in nurses in general, worsened by the fact that fewer students were graduating from nursing schools. Through my collaborator, I gained access to an informed person within the company and continued my questioning and research preparation for the initial meeting.

EASE PAIN POINTS

I developed a strong value proposition to help the company by demonstrating how its recruitment issue affected earnings per share (EPS). Further, I documented how my company could improve its EPS by 20 to 30 percent by reducing nurse turnover. I calculated turnover rates and training costs studied how competitors solved the issue, and recommended solutions with sustainable advantages. Get to the CEO's pain point, then get to your value.

Begin by gathering pertinent information on your prospect's business and industry position. Probe for information based on his or her priorities, insofar as you can know them at this point. Draw a general industry or sector profile, fleshing out key developments, innovations, inventory status, supply chain vitality, and risk management issues. Identify revenue, credit or funding challenges. Be on the lookout for emerging opportunities where you could bring value.

A simple formula for research: Zoom in on what keeps the CEO up at night. By studying the Letter to Shareholders in the company's annual report, you can pluck out gems between the lines. These public statements reveal mission, values and strategic direction and detail financial performance, even competitive strategy. Once you become adept at this process, create a data template to profile all the players in a sector, because these issues are common across thousands of companies.

A wealth of information is available in the trade press, both in print and online. There are nearly 20,000 magazines published in America alone, and hundreds of thousands of niche websites that serve as excellent portals to more background than you can ever dream to absorb. Not sure which media outlets are important? Consult the *Journal of Trade Journals* at the library. Search for articles with contrarian viewpoints and balance your findings against conventional wisdom. Strive for a well-rounded viewpoint of your own.

OPPORTUNITY LIST

As you read, keep a pad of paper handy, your Opportunity List. Or take notes on your iPad, laptop or smart phone. Use some type of device as a repository for your thoughts. We need technical backup for memory worn down by information overload. When you run across a key business issue, write it down. Formulate these sub-issues into primary and secondary headings. For example, an employee turnover problem falls under Reducing Corporate Cost or Improving Competitive Posture. Refer to your Opportunity List daily and, as you do, the synapses will fire and you will formulate creative approaches to prospect problems.

Use the power of the Internet to fine-tune your research antennae. You will gather much of the financial information you need from the company's website. Naturally, public companies are easier to research than private ones. Also Edgar's, Hoovers, FreeERISA, and KnowX are comprehensive sources for public information. For an extra boost, visit www.primere-source.com for valuable links to popular information resources. For topical news via corporate press releases, create a Google Alert to search on key words. Spiders comb the web and Google responds with feedback in a timely email.

LinkedIn is another valuable research tool on the Internet. It is easy to navigate, offers robust functionality, and membership is inexpensive. Type in a company name and get a jackpot of information. You will learn what links you share with others in the organization, who has recently joined the company, its competitors, and who else is searching or linking themselves to that company. LinkedIn is today's online equivalent to a corporate mixer or networking event. In fact, LinkedIn works well as a branding and networking channel. More on this later.

You should also see if the company has a fan page on Facebook, a valuable resource for learning what clients are saying about their providers.

Before I dig into the research on my targeted company, I use a valuable web-based tool designed by a Texas company First Research. First Research www.firstresearch.com offers a unique tool to explore the opportunities hidden in more than 900 industry segments. First Research is one of the leading providers of market analysis tools to enable sales and marketing teams perform faster and smarter. This tool has helped me open more doors and close more sales more quickly. It has also help to cut my research time in half. Let me give you an example of my preparation for a client in the healthcare industry.

My prospect was a Fortune 500 healthcare provider, operating more than 50 hospitals nationwide. By going to First Research's industry profile page, I was able to zero in on hospitals. I clicked "industry audio podcast" where I listened to a three-minute industry overview. As a result, I had clear snapshot of industry structure, competitive landscape, regional and international issues, key performance and economic indicators, monthly news and quarterly updates.

First Research complements the MERGE Process with a deep level of detail, key concerns and actual questions to ask the CEO, CFO, CIO and executives in human resources, information technology and marketing and sales. Once I add myself to the email alert, I receive regular updates on whatever industry I am following. I encourage you to take full advantage of this valuable research tool.

Here is a selective list of other useful resources to help you ace the research srep of the MERGE consulting process:

Annual Reports

The Letter to Shareholders is worth close examination. You will learn past corporate performance, planned strategic direction, vision and values, and hints at the culture. The language used in the letter can handily reveal the corporate personality. If the CEO refers to his employees as "associates," do not call them employees. If the CEO refers to his company as the market leader, find out why and which companies hold the second and third tiers.

The full report packages the income statement, balance sheet, management discussion and analysis, stock-related information, as well as the key executive and director details. Do a search to determine if these individuals sit on boards of other companies and how that might impact your relationship development process.

10K/10Q Reports

This report is required of all publicly traded companies by the Securities and Exchange Commission (SEC), and is chock full of valuable information. In addition to discovering helpful bits such as corporate strategy and competitive standing, you will find a listing of documents ranging from employment contracts and deferred compensation plans to stock option agreements and leases. Equally importantly, the 10K lists corporate risk factors. Your value proposition can close the gap. The 10Q is a quarterly version of the 10k, also required by the SEC.

8Q Reports

These official reports inform shareholders about any significant changes that may affect the company, such as a new president, acquisitions, mergers, and other information.

Proxy Reports

Generated annually, proxy reports offer additional information not found elsewhere, including compensation levels for the top five executives, their stock holdings, backgrounds on board members and a summary of executive benefits.

Company Collateral Material

The way a company communicates to the market reveals its corporate personality and brand platform. If you invest the time to review every piece of external literature you will be pleasantly surprised by the powerful information waiting to be harvested. For instance, recruiting materials deliver company overviews, snapshots on philosophies and assessments of strengths and opportunities. Product literature provides insight into engineering principles, the role of innovation, product and market applications, and basic marketing and sales strategy.

Corporate advertising, when executed well, showcases the soul of the brand and how the company hopes to be perceived by the marketplace. News releases are filled with topical details to chart direction, competitive posture and market leadership. Become a sponge. A moment will occur in that initial meeting when remembering the right word or fact or positioning statement may save the day.

U.S. Industrial Outlook

U.S. Industrial Outlook is a publication of the U.S. Department of Commerce's International Trade Administration and provides coverage and analysis of United States business and industry. Here you will find the background, the outlook, the trends, the problems, and the opportunities of 250 different industries.

Standard and Poor's Industry Surveys

Standard & Poor's Industry Surveys is considered the fast track to industry knowledge on more than 50 of the largest North American and global industries. Reports are written by an industry research analyst on key areas of interest: Current Environment, Industry Trends, How the Industry Operates, Key Industry Ratios and Statistics, How to Analyze a Company, even a Glossary of Industry Terms. http://sandp.ecnext.com/coms2/page_industry

Value Line Investment Survey

Regarded as the gold standard in investment research, this resource gives you facts, dollars, trends, and business projections for 1,700 companies—far more information than the average employee knows about her own company. http://www.valueline.com/Products.

Dominant Trade or Association Magazine for Prospect's Industry

Arrive early at your initial meeting and discover the publications your prospect values right on the lobby coffee table. If you read the editorial page, you can grasp quickly the burning issue of the day in your prospect or client's industry.

Research Private Companies

Unlike public companies, private companies are not required to file with the Securities and Exchange Commission (SEC). Important information to be found in these documents is not readily available for private companies. Dig a little digger and you may find what you need on the company website, LinkedIn or in trade articles. Also, refer to Dun & Bradstreet reports, local business journals, and Hoover's Handbook of Private Companies. Good information is housed at the office of the Secretary of State as companies are required to file standard business documents. The National Association of Secretaries of State offers an easy pull down menu to find your state's website. Weber State University's website provides a library with a research guide for private company resources. Go to http://library.weber.edu/cm/business/private.cfm.

Colleges and Universities

One of the most overlooked information resources is your own alumni group. Many major universities store large amounts of well-sourced research data. I have found this information very helpful in supporting many of the concepts I present.

Hire Your Own Research Team

There are many small firms in your area that specialize in research. They even have their own club, the Association of Independent Information Professionals, with over 300 members. Ask your local librarian for the *Directory of Associations*.

Internal and External "Insiders"

Many individuals inside and outside the prospect organization possess unpublished information. For example, if you speak to established vendors to the company, you can learn about the political landscape, the decision making process, corporate culture, quirks in personalities, and more.

If your product is designed to improve sales productivity, talk to someone in the field who sells for the company. If your service is purely a CEO buy, carefully find a discreet way to speak with his contacts at charity events, golf outings or fraternal gatherings. Preferably, speak to someone informally at a much lower level than the target prospect you intend to call on. You definitely want to minimize any social faux pas or breach in privacy or protocol.

Connect the dots on all these sources of information, and you will organically paint a revealing portrait of the prospect, industry, and competitor positions. Only then are salespeople fully equipped to craft solutions that address prospect priorities, solve problems, and bring measurable value.

Fact gathering is essential for two reasons. First, facts compensate for a lack of gut instinct and stop you from winging your approach to a company. If you initiate discussions with ample knowledge on your prospect's situation, you give yourself a priceless advantage. Second, facts bridge the credibility gap. When you sell to top executives, especially if you are younger in age, the CEO or CFO will not place much credence in your message unless you are well prepared with facts to back you up.

I encourage you to research the prospect's largest competitors as thoroughly as you research the prospect. When working with the prospect, mentally sit on the same side of the table and rally against the competitor. Demonstrate an understanding of how the opponent's behavior affects the prospect's business. Perhaps the competition is using unfair pricing tactics, buying market share, or selling product knock-offs. Genuinely empathize with your prospect and see the world through his or her eyes. And you may be paid the ultimate compliment: "You understand our business." Now you have relegated your competitor to vendor status and elevated yourself to the realm of partner.

FEAR FACTOR

Know that there is also a dark side to good research. Prospects can actually fear the power of information. If they are confronted too directly with the facts they—or someone above them—might not like what they see. This is a risk. Tread lightly. But if you discover that a company has a major employee turnover problem or revenues lag in the face of poor incentive programs, and your solution fits, you have done the company a valuable service.

One way to blunt the fear factor is to survey and benchmark peer companies around sought-after performance indicators. Become the go-to resource for quality data. Show companies how they stack up against the competition. Companies covet competitive intelligence. Years ago, my company at the time created a national survey on executive benefits in the Fortune 1000, and many companies used this data to benchmark themselves against best practices. Still today, competitors reference that survey in their own reports, which helps to tag you as a thought leader.

Now that you accept the research mindset, allow me to introduce The Law of Unpredictability, one of *The 22 Immutable Laws of Marketing* by Al Ries and Jack Trout. By its nature, research measures the past. It does not predict the future. Often, prospects simply do not know what they will do when confronted with a problem or decision. How do you get around this?

Study the trends, learn to forecast or study those who do. But build into your planning a large dose of flexibility, adaptability and what-if scenarios. We are imperfect beings who think and act in "predictably irrational" ways.

The takeaway? Prepare extensively in advance of your initial call, build a winning solution backed with facts, and increase your probability of closing the sale. Thorough preparation and advance planning are common traits in top performers, and the architectural detail of flawless execution.

6 | MULTIPLE DECISION MAKERS

Getting to Yes

Complex sales are conceptual events requiring the buy-in of multiple influencers, each with their own vested interest in the outcome. The entire C-level executive team may participate. Heads of line departments may join in. Board level approval may be required. Trusted outsiders may be asked to weigh in on final decisions. Complex sales are called such because they present an intricate puzzle of interlocking *human* pieces that are inherently subject to change.

In a complex sale, the decision making cycle can unfold over many months or many years. Dollar values are typically high. The risk of making a wrong decision poses a greater threat to decision makers. Illustrative examples range from enterprise-wide software conversions or building new manufacturing facilities to employee benefits or training programs.

In a complex sale, the buying process is actually a long chain of inter-related decisions, heavily layered and nuanced, that can emanate from anywhere in the client organization. The professional services consultant must respect the absolute need for deep research at the 30,000-foot-level, as well as down into the trenches. How else will you know that the General Counsel has ultimate veto power, or that an outside accountant is well connected with a board member and can advance your agenda? [Chart 11]

Every organization you approach is comprised of a colorful tapestry of individuals with surprisingly different levels of influence and decision making authority. Carefully study all the buying influences and their agendas, insofar as you can uncover them. It always astonishes me when the CEO who, in our minds, is in full control is influenced by a lower-level employee, even an executive assistant. Trust me; I was bewildered once or twice early in my career by the outside power curve of some innocuous person who ended up sandbagging a deal. I learned to master this over the years by improving my ability to build and leverage all of the buying influences in a complex sale. This chapter will give you a road map to help speed up your sales cycle.

Chart 11
Identify Roles

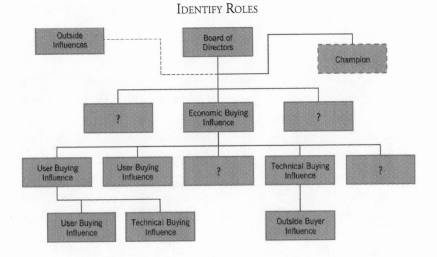

Skilled Facilitation

To build consensus with individuals in groups and prevent being undermined by an unknown antagonist, I urge you to study the art of skilled facilitation. Typically, the facilitator of a group will be neutral, with no decision making authority, and is acceptable to all the members of the group. You can assume this role, but only as a problem solver and solution finder. Recognize that in many organizations, the decision making process is not always clear, and people may not even understand their own role in group dynamics, or if there is a group at all. Groupthink, unfortunately, is crippling to companies, especially when it begins to polarize an entire organization. Tread lightly.

Skilled facilitation begins by understanding the archetypes in a group. I recommend keeping it simple, and please know that these are my unscientific definitions; however, they are referred to in the thousands-of-years-old Enneagram, which maps out nine fundamental personality types of human nature and how they interrelate. Enneagram profiling follows a unique set of questions, which we do not have space for in this text. See if you can't find yourself in one of these informal and extremely brief descriptions:

1. **The Reformer.** Often a principled and responsible leader, with a crusader's zeal, the reformer can come off as self-righteous, contradictory and inflexible. Sound like anyone you know? A COO or head of engineering.

2. **The Helper.** As the name implies, the helper is quite supportive and you want her on your side, but she can be manipulative and overbearing. Handle with caution. She may occupy the HR office.

3. **The Achiever.** Many CEOs are achievers and success-oriented motivators. They are image-conscious and bent on self-improvement. At worst, they can be self-promoting, opportunistic and relentless. American business rewards these traits.

4. **The Individualist.** Many of us strive to be individualists. These types tend to be life-enhancing, creative and introspective. However, under stress, they can be borderline self-indulgent and may be temperamental. Do I see a VP of marketing?

5. **The Investigator.** Fives are visionaries, usually focused and observant, well-prepared, a little detached and preoccupied. CFOs lean in this direction and often can be the technical or economic buyers in your multi-decision mix.

6. **The Loyalist.** Everyone wants this personality type on their team. Reliable, committed, cooperative, and often courageous, a loyalist in your court could tip the sale. But be aware, under stress, they can panic and fall apart.

7. **The Enthusiast.** Sevens are the energy spark in the group. Their productive nature and fully engaged style can rally the group. But they are prone to over-talking, distraction and self-centeredness under stress. I see this type in a lot of sales roles.

8. **The Challenger.** Challengers can be found in the C-Suites and in board members. They are strong, self-confident and pragmatic and, on the flip side, can be confrontational and intimidating. These people are often seen as gatekeepers or technical buyers. They can say no, but they can't say yes.

9. **The Peacemaker.** Often unselfish individuals, nines place great importance on inner stability and harmony. Be careful, however, as they may become complacent and disengage. Collaborators as well as board members may express this type.

Unless you are permitted to profile everyone on the decision tree with the Enneagram, you can't possibly know their personality type. However, you can learn to read personalities through verbal and visual cues. Identify the personalities up front, as much as possible. Collaborate according to type. Let the Enthusiast talk. Give the Investigator all the facts he needs. Reaffirm the Helper and so on. Then strive to guide the whole "rattling caravan" of decision makers from a respectable distance.

In today's world, most decisions result from a consensus-building effort, which only adds to the complexity. Because of this, I find our MERGE Process is effective in pulling forward certain decision makers, based on involvement with the ultimate purchase of our services.

MAGNIFICENT SEVEN

A study by Wesley J. Jonson of Ohio State University and Thomas V. Bonoma of the Harvard Business School found that for major product purchases, there was an average of seven decision makers. For a major services purchase, there was an average of five decision makers. Successful salespeople prepare a strategy to cover each of these decision makers because if the decision making and approval process is a mystery, you will not land the business. Here's what you need to find out:

- How do decisions get made for your product or service?
- What process did the company undertake when it chose the incumbent?
- How many decision makers are there? Who are they?
- Who are the people who influence them?
- Who are the key gatekeepers?
- Who is the primary decision maker?
- What are the individual "wins" each decision maker has?

In *Dirty Little Secrets*, Sharon Drew Morgen recommends assembling the "Buying Team" as early as possible to move your prospect forward quickly. She recommends asking up front:

- Have you ever done anything like this before? If so, how did you find the right people to involve? And what from that process can you use here? If not, what would you need to consider helping your internal folks know that something like we're suggesting would support your business objectives?
- At what point would you recognize all the past initiatives, departments, and vendors that have maintained your status quo and would need to buy in to change in order for you to move forward?
- Once the Buying Team is fully formed, what would you need to consider, given your status quo, to know how to move forward in such a way that you don't meet resistance?
- How could you all move together, one step at a time, so that you could create a workable plan in a manageable time scale?
- What would you need to see from me to help you get where you need to be? And at what point would you need me to support your internal buy-in efforts?

Most salespeople don't ask these questions. Morgen's research shows that by using these facilitative type questions, you can slash your sales cycles significantly.

Bonoma, in partnership with Benson Shapiro of the Harvard Business School, described the different roles of the players in purchase situations in the book *Segmenting the Industrial Market*. Later, Robert Miller and Stephen Heiman simplified the concept in their book *Strategic Selling*. Using ideas from this research, we developed a process to map these decision makers, which you can use in each of your prospect companies.

Six basic types of decision makers collectively define the buying center for the majority of decisions surrounding financial or professional services. [Chart 12]

CHART 12

BUYING CENTERS

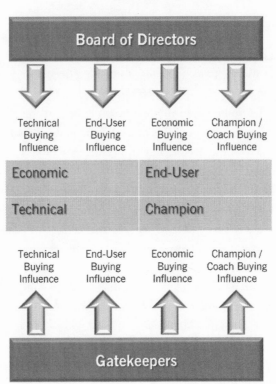

Economic Buyer

The economic buyer is one individual or a group of several contributors to the decision who holds direct access to budgets and the authority to release funds. This individual also has veto power and will exercise that power often, without regard to the decisions or desires of the other members in the decision making process.

But the economic buyer is difficult to identify. Many speculate his identity at the wrong level in the organization. In fact, a fair number of my consultants over the years were led to believe they connected with the money source, only to be proven wrong after months of wasted effort. Let me give you an example from one of my organizations.

A few years ago I was playing golf in one of my club's member-guest tournaments when we were teamed up with a guy who sold quite complex copying and publishing equipment. I really had a great time with this individual, and his rapport building skills gave me the feeling I had known him all of my life. He then asked me what type of equipment we used (wrong question) and wanted to come see me to explain what his company did. He assumed for this type of purchase, I was the economic buyer since I was CEO.

I hate to admit it in writing, but I did not know what we had or whether we owned it, leased it or even the current cost. These decisions were all made by my CFO and are a part of our budgeting process. My only interest is what they do, how they improve our image, and how they can improve our success rate and increase the firm's revenues. Quite frankly, this great guy should have focused on his value proposition and done a lot more research on my company and situation.

Focused Prospects

As you will learn later, I probably should have been viewed as an end-user buyer and could have been his champion. I sent him to my CFO, who saw him as someone trying to sell the benefits and features of his product when we realized there was no need for his services.

Unfortunately, his timing wasn't good either, as everyone in the company was busy on other projects, which seems to be the case even with my own prospects. Busy people don't have time for things that aren't urgent; it's too much work. Whenever you approach your prospect with features and benefits, he looks at the status quo and makes a decision on whether to invest the time.

I learned from my own experience in this situation. Prospects really focus on three distinct decisions when approached by you or your competitors:

1. They first evaluate how you approached them to determine if it is worth investing their time to meet with you. Remember, like my CFO, people are busy and their time is valuable.

2. Most decisions require some change, and change is a hard thing to do. They evaluate your value proposition to determine if it is worth the disruption to make a change.

3. And finally, they want to think of all of the alternatives and they want to make sure they are selecting the best option for their situation. This is why a collaborative process with key decision makers is important.

All three of these decisions involve multiple decision makers and personal decisions by various influences. Knowing who has what power is key.

Don't allow yourself to be sidetracked. People often try to impress others by implying they have more control and decision making authority than they actually do. To counteract this problem, we charge minimal fees for our initial consulting work. If your contact does not have authority to pay for an initial study, she will not be in a position to buy the total solution. What's more, the initial study enables you to get "under the tent" and continue to identify the decision makers.

Understandably then, it is essential to ask during your initial meeting, "What is the decision making and approval process?" Listen carefully to the answer and how those in attendance describe the process. Listen for what is not being said, as well. Interestingly, the final individual discussed in the process is typically your economic decision maker.

When you are in front of this person, verify his role by simply asking: 1) "Will you make the final recommendation or give the final approval?"; 2) "Is there anyone else in the organization who can veto this project?"

The answers will lead you directly to your intended outcome. And your questioning is not overly assertive or pushy. Smart businesspeople expect you to be efficient and use their time well. Ask the right questions of the right people and you will build respect.

TEAM VICTORY

In my experience, present to the economic buyer first by offering her information with a direct impact on corporate performance. This approach produces a victory for the entire decision team and is more likely to advance your cause.

For example, when I first research an opportunity, I review the key initiatives and risk factors in the organization or industry so I can clearly determine the impact of change or status quo. If I have a piece of information to use that also impacts the economic buyer personally, all the better.

If I miss the mark by failing to grasp their desired results and some of the alternatives to the status quo as an initial discussion point, I risk being sent to a lower level player with no expressed interest from the top. In my example above, the equipment salesman should have focused on our consulting process and how his equipment could improve deliverables to our clients and improve our image, revenue and bottom line. Ideally, you want the economic decision maker to champion your effort as early as possible in the sales cycle, but you need to give them a reason to do so.

It is not uncommon to hold a high-level strategic discussion with the economic buyer, or someone close to that level, and sell them on your value proposition to improve their current situation, only to get the process pushed down a level or two in order to kick-start the engagement. When this happens—and it will happen often—it is very important for you to map out why your prospect needs to have an internal team with various disciplines go through your process. I always try to stay connected to the economic buyer. Let me give you another example.

Recently, I was introduced to the CEO of a multibillion-dollar New York Stock Exchange food company. I did my homework and saw several areas to guide my initial discussions. On my first call, he tried to send me down to the director of human resources; however, I discussed with him that I had researched his company and found several areas where we could improve his competitive position, as well as support some of his key initiatives.

I emphasized to the CEO, "If you decide to invite me back after our initial meeting, I think it will be important for me to work with your human resource director, as well as others, but first I wanted to meet to make sure you feel we could bring some value." He agreed to meet.

I mentioned key points I read in his annual report from his letter to the shareholders, where he cited the need to expand retail locations, reduce operating cost, provide make-a-difference incentives to his people, and become a world-class organization. I shared with him a peer analysis to show where his competitors stood, and how they were succeeding at attracting and retaining their key people. I also used examples of how we have helped companies in similar situations and asked him to describe the three biggest challenges his company is facing right now in reaching its business goals. He responded:

1. Find the right talent to manage his new store expansion. (I probed further to understand what he was currently doing and considering. I learned he was using a recruiting firm, what it meant from a revenue standpoint to find these people, and how his growth plans would stall if he didn't recruit and retain the right people.)

2. Improve shareholder value by increasing the earnings per share, which was part of his quest for reducing cost. (Again, I probed further to better understand what this meant.)

3. Find the right incentives to align his people with corporate objectives. (With more questioning, I understood his thinking.)

Again, I shared various examples of how we helped others in a similar situation and suggested possible alternatives, and then focused on our collaborative process, explaining how we find solutions that others may have overlooked.

I sensed he was impressed and wanted to take this to the next step, so I suggested a meeting with his team (the other decision makers) that he would assign to such a project. It was very important that he attend the next meeting, so I could feed back to him and the group his key objectives, using his own words.

GET THE YES

It is important to understand the multiple points of contact and what agendas they hold, as well as their personal wins. You need to continue to involve this group, both people inside and outside the company, throughout your entire process. Not everyone on this team can say "yes" and make a sale happen, but everyone on this team can say "no" and make a sale more difficult. In my experience the final decision maker rarely overrides the majority.

Whether you sell to high-net worth individuals or are involved in a transaction with an individual, there still are buying influences to consider. On a purchase of real estate, you and your spouse may be the economic buyers, but you listen to your accountant, lawyer, financial advisor, and even the kids for the final decision. Let's take a moment to review the classic decision maker roles.

END-USER BUYER

Typically, there are multiple end users in any given company for financial products or professional services. Their paramount concern is how your solution impacts their job performance.

In my business, the end users are executives enrolled in our programs; human resource professionals responsible for administration; finance staff who oversee funding, and others who could play a major role. Recently, in one engagement, the IT department played a key role because it had serious concerns with the time required to convert their payroll systems to our program. In this case, the IT department could also be considered a technical buyer, which we will discuss shortly.

In a recent situation, I thought the human resource person was acting as a gatekeeper. She was not on board with my recommended solution and had influenced the CEO that ours was not the right timing because the company was busy working other projects. I failed to find out her personal win and later found out she had her own budget issues. She saw our program as an administrative and cost burden to her department. She was seriously understaffed and, in her mind, she could not dedicate more resources to our proposed project. She had done so two years earlier and did not wish to revisit it again so soon.

FAMILIAR VS. NEW

I empathized with her situation and told her I understood her position exactly. I asked a series of questions to determine what would be her ideal outcome, short of not doing anything. I learned she was a big fan of consolidating services and vendors, and would prefer to deal with their current 401(k) provider and their system. Her position is common among end-user buyers; it is always easier for them to add on to an existing program, process, or technology than to justify something entirely new.

Not wishing to give up, I spent the time to demonstrate how our program could be implemented seamlessly for her, and how our team could make her work life better. We had our team members spend more time with her and other buying influences within the company itself. You need to spot these situations early, before it is too late for the economic buyers; they rarely reverse their decisions. Often in situations like this, you need to look for ways to coexist with your prospects' behavior, while addressing their needs.

As you can see, end users raise their own questions, which can improve or detract from the sales climate. They want to know if your proposal, and ultimate outcome, adds to their workload, costs them coveted resources, or affects other initiatives underway. An end user can construct a road block to your effort because he does not want to deal with a new firm, and he may fight hard to retain the incumbent. It is a common challenge I face. While he is unlikely to make the decision alone, his support for any initiative is essential. Focus on making their lives simpler.

For instance, in my example above, if a company has a relationship with an existing 401(k) provider, yet knows it needs the new nonqualified plan you propose, it may simply prefer to add the new plan to the same vendor platform—despite your superior system. People don't embrace change well. Like all of us, end users want to simplify their lives and not add more work.

Obviously, you want to address these concerns up front and demonstrate ease of implementation and ease of use, or show the end user a numbers-driven business case that captures and solves his concerns. Do all of this without a single untoward word about the existing provider, and the end user will draw his own conclusions. The next decision point person is one of the most coveted.

THE CHAMPION

Every situation must have someone who will take responsibility and help champion your product or service through the decision making process. By far, the champion is one of the most important roles in the decision making process in an organization. Typically, champions have a stake in the game from a financial standpoint and are personally interested in getting the boss what she wants.

The champion can help you understand the decision-making and approval process and coach you along the way. She will basically tell you what needs to be done and who you need to satisfy in order to get the final decision to move forward.

This person can come from any level within or outside the organization and must be identified early in your process. Don't expect them to raise their hand and volunteer for this role; you must dig deep and find them, and they are in all buying situations.

Early in the process, you might ask the group, "How are decisions made and how do things work around the company?" Listen for the person who seems to be the most informed and who has an individual win in the situation. Your goal is to select this person and work closely with him or her to learn as much as possible about the company, its people and personal wins. I want my champion to help me minimize or eliminate the "no" votes when the decisions are made. Champions are a wealth of information and can tell you which ideas not to bring up, which words not to use, or which people you need to satisfy, as well as how to position your value proposition.

In my end-user example with the HR person, I first went to my champion to ask why the HR department was not on board with my recommendations. He told me that she had been under a lot of stress lately due to personnel cutbacks in her department, and she did not feel her voice was heard on the committee. He suggested that I invite her to lunch or coffee and get to know her as a person, listen to her concerns, and make her feel part of the process. He also volunteered to have the CFO, who was on board with the recommendations, let her know how important it was to him personally and to the company.

Ultimately, she became a champion, improving our success and shortening our sales cycle. Anyone can be your champion. In a perfect world, you may find your champion in the same role as the economic buyer. Now let's move on to the technical buyer.

TECHNICAL BUYER

The technical buyer is the person or persons who may not be able to give you a yes, but they certainly can say no (and usually do). Saying no represents power to them. The technical buyer loves facts, data, numbers, statistics, peer analysis, and is frequently enamored with technology for technology's sake. Many times, these buyers run the Request for Proposal process, which you need to avoid.

In my world, the technical buyers are the benefit specialists in accounting, personnel in finance and HR and, in some cases, outside advisors like in accounting and law firms. For you, the technical buyer could be the manager of sales support in the regional offices, or the production chief in manufacturing. They all represent influencers who can improve or detract from your ultimate objective. That is why it pays to carefully think through the impact of your proposal on all the operating units within an organization.

If you make contact with the technical buyer first, you run the risk of getting trapped into a product evaluation that could lead to a competitive assessment. You will be unable to move beyond him without creating the impression you went over his head, freezing your process in its tracks. While technical buyer generally cannot—or will not—make a decision, she is often there to verify the technical aspects of your recommendation and not to help you push things through, unless it can be seen as major win for the technical team.

When you target a company at the most senior level, you will often be shuffled off to the technical buyer who handles your area of expertise. He knows exactly the person to whom you should speak and is eager to transfer the call. Avoid this. Don't assume this is a way into the company; hold out for someone at the decision making level. It will be well worth the wait. If you are in the employee benefits business or selling financial planning services, your contact will assume that you should be talking to someone in HR. The larger the company, the more politics and turf protection exist. Few employees openly want to step on someone else's toes.

When I am consulting, I enter the company at the CFO level and focus on an issue of personal impact, not the technical aspects of my product. If the CFO sees a personal win, when he takes a technical viewpoint, as he is bound to do, he will help justify cost verses status quo. Let me give you an example.

In one engagement, my targeted company provided motivation to its senior executives with stock options and restricted stock units and had implemented stock ownership guidelines. These guidelines were developed to require the management team to own a certain percentage of its compensation in company stock.

When I examined the CFO's personal situation, outlined in the company's proxy statement, I calculated his personal income tax exposure to conform to the guidelines. My solution could reduce this cost with no additional cost to the company. When I approached him, I focused on his personal situation, and then discussed the cost-neutral aspects to the company. Naturally, he was very interested in his personal situation and therefore motivated to invest the time to understand the accounting and tax aspects to the company.

GATEKEEPERS

Gatekeepers are the crossing guards of corporate life, and they can kill your deal. They are found inside or outside the company and among all buying influences. They play a pivotal role in the due diligence process because it is often their responsibility to protect access to the decision making team and, in the extreme, to uncover issues with your product or service. Economic buyers rely on them to expose the pitfalls. The gatekeeper may be a trusted assistant, a business friend or an outside advisor.

To neutralize the influence of a gatekeeper, form a network of key collaborators in whose interest it is to keep the buying decision moving in your direction. As an example, finance executives inside the company can be gatekeepers, but they will turn to their auditors for technical support and advice. If you have experience with their auditors, you can cover a lot of ground in advance. Legal staff inside the company can be gatekeepers and will look to outside counsel for support and advice. Next, let's examine the role of boards of directors.

BOARD OF DIRECTORS

In most large organizations, especially those with a focus on good corporate governance, boards of directors play a major role in the decision making process. Many times the final decision is technically made by the board itself. In fact, the members of the board play the same four buying roles as discussed above. In my world, the compensation committee of the board ultimately stamps its approval on our recommendations before the entire board votes.

Understand early in your process how much influence the board wields. Determine if there are key members of the board who could roadblock your progress. During your research, find out what other boards the members sit on and what roles they hold in their own organizations. Find out their collaborators and how you can involve them in your process. Your designated champion can help answer a great many strategic questions about the board's involvement.

Let's assume you've done all your homework and mapped out a fairly reliable assessment of the decision making process in your prospect organization. You are confident and keep moving forward. What can go wrong?

FIRE ALARMS

In 2006, the Harvard Business School produced a study, "Sales Reps' Biggest Mistakes," which measured what clients really think about the salespeople who come through their doors. Harvard surveyed 138 clients responsible for making business-to-business purchases for large North American companies in a multitude of industries. The results were eye-opening.

Note the list of grievances in the pie chart below. Chief among them are poor listening skills and the salesperson's (or consultant's) failure to follow client buying processes. [Chart 13]

CHART 13

THE PROBLEM WITH SALESPEOPLE

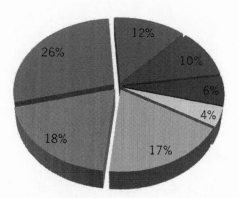

- 17% - Don't follow up
- 18% - Don't listen to my needs
- 26% - Don't follow my company's buying process
- 12% - Are pushy, aggressive, or disrespectful
- 10% - Don't explain solutions adequately
- 6% - Make exaggerated or inaccurate claims
- 4% - Don't understand my business

In your quest for success, if you do nothing else but **learn to listen and follow the client buying process**, you eliminate half the reason why clients say no. To this end, I'd like to recommend the book *Just Listen*, by the distinguished consultant, business coach and psychiatrist Mark Goulston, M.D. Also, I encourage you to embrace the concepts in this chapter on multiple decision makers. You will be well on your way to cracking the code of the complex sale.

7 | MARKETING COMMUNICATIONS
Promoting Your Firm's Value

"There is no doubt that if marketing were done perfectly, selling, in the actual sense of the word, would be unnecessary."

—Peter Drucker

There are few things in this world that approach perfection except, perhaps, the love of a child and the beauty of Nature. Certainly, little or nothing about marketing is perfect. It is messy, often imprecise, and seemingly unpredictable. Despite this reality, I am going to attempt in this chapter to lay down a basic, get-you-started foundation for marketing communications—one to set you and your firm apart in a sea of choice for professional services.

Effective marketing communications is a multi-pronged, integrated process. No one marketing action will do it all. Effective marketing takes a complete strategy and coordinated effort to influence the buyer's ultimate decision, backed by tailored tools and techniques that closely reflect buyer perspectives and preferences for information.

MERGE Forward

As you think about how to promote your firm, avoid launching into your marketing campaign until your prospect's decision making process and buying process are indelibly etched in your mind. Research solid data to help you highlight the major issues your profile prospect faces. Then define a winning value proposition and organize your marketing activity to support it, always coordinating your solution into your overall message. Weave this point of view into your promotion plan, and give your prospects a means to self-discover that yours is the best and only logical solution.

If you do not define the decision and buying process in advance, and etch them in stone, you will cast about in confusion. If you do not lay out your differentiation and value proposition in advance of launching a marketing communication plan, it is as foolhardy as making a cross-country trip without a map.

Surprisingly, many firms send out mixed messages to external audiences. Their public relations, brochures, articles or advertising communicate a disconnect between intention and outcome. You have undoubtedly witnessed this yourself. Consider how one firm hails its customer service on radio, but its website emphasizes product features. Another firm may claim a brand position built on innovation, yet it has not introduced a new product in five years. Consistency of message is critical to effective marketing communications.

In our experience, there are six structural posts around which to build and promote your firm's value: [Chart 14]
1. Marketing education
2. Online presence
3. Leverage marketing
4. Indirect promotion
5. Advisory boards
6. Paid advertising

MARKETING EDUCATION

To sell a complex product or service, you need to cultivate educated buyers, who become better equipped to understand your differentiation. I call this education-based marketing, and it is organized around your core marketing message. Importantly, these messages must be delivered or embedded in higher-order written materials, articles, quotes in newspapers, reports, white papers, advertising, seminars, newsletters and online videos, and should reinforce your Internet strategy.

CHART 14
PROMOTING YOUR FIRM'S VALUES

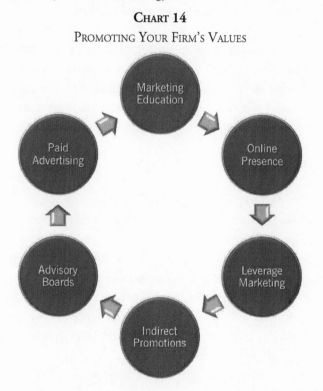

The key to education-based marketing is subordination of sales messaging. Inform, inspire and seek to influence. Don't sell. Allow your prospect to self-discover your solution with an informational message. An educational-based approach to marketing communications offers a library of benefits:

- You create a flow of information that helps prospects seek you out
- You give prospects what they want: Knowledge
- You reach prospects at stage one in their interest in the subject
- You inform and advise, removing the prospect's discomfort at being sold

- You are viewed as a professional advisor versus a salesman
- You establish yourself as an authority on the subject
- You save prospects time and money in research
- You create a positive experience with your firm

In short, education-based marketing captures prospective clients earlier in the decision making process, establishes a relationship of trust, and results in higher closing ratios. This same educational strategy should be extended to your client's advisor network—the collaborators in the Five Cs. Everyone who influences your client's decision should be educated.

ONLINE PRESENCE

I learned early on to use the websites of my businesses as interactive information centers, rather than simply to create online brochures. With RCG, 18,000 people registered in our "knowledge center," to gain access to webcasts, articles, reports and a rich array of free content. An active, vibrant and value-generating website is the cornerstone of your marketing communications effort. It is your billboard in cyberspace, and it will attract traffic (and leads) if done well. To ensure we segment correctly, we developed a variety of various landing pages to attract different prospects interested in a broad range of subjects.

Begin with a clear web strategy and identify one or more targeted audiences. The most important thing to remember as you develop your online line marketing strategy is to put your products and services to the side for a little while and focus your complete attention on the client of your product or service (or those who will be collaborators). Remember to focus on value proposition and not products and services. I know this is difficult for many, but it will pay off by bringing you closer to achieving your firm's goals.

In my opinion, many firms are focused on the wrong measures of success with their online strategy. Most people focus on traffic. Traffic is the wrong measurement. Instead, lead the visitors to where they can help you reach your true goals, driving more revenue and profit to your firm. Use your site to help educate people, which is an important element in the early stages of their buying process.

The Internet has become a useful tool for executives to find information. Forbes Insight, in association with Google, recently released a new study called *The Rise of the Digital C-Suite: How Executives Locate and Filter Business Information.* According to the study, the respondents rated the Internet as very valuable in searching business data needed to make decisions.

Understand up front how much time you want to invest in your web footprint. How often are you willing to update content? What type of content is valued by what type of client or prospect? My goals have always been to create a marketing machine that generates high activity and brand awareness, and to focus on clients seeing us as a valuable resource. The more clicks, the greater exposure, but that is not the goal. The goal is to attract the right people who buy and support our targeted markets. We updated frequently with relevant content to ensure visitors kept coming back and stayed on the site long enough to internalize our value proposition. There are many tools available to help you monitor this activity.

Relevant content that is well organized and keyword rich attracts the search engines and, ideally, the self-qualified leads you need. If you publish interesting content, people read it and pass it along to friends, clients and associates. Make it easy for visitors to register on your site; your forms should be simple and request little more than a name and email address. We reinforced this registration by offering our visitors our quarterly magazine and invitations to webcasts or special events.

Add white papers to your web presence. When you produce and post a white paper to your site, it has a magnetizing effect on interested visitors. Google "white paper on" and enter your subject matter, amazing listings pop up. "White papers typically argue a specific position or solution to a problem," according to Michael A. Stelzner, author of *Writing White Papers.* Use his resource as a launch page.

Today, all of us are wrapped in a brave, new social web where relationships take on immediate connectedness, where news and content travel in real time, and where search engine optimization is hard currency. Pre-web, there were only a handful of ways to tell your story. You could buy advertising, which was expensive; hire a PR firm to get you ink, or put the feet on the ground and build a national sales force, also both expensive. The Internet is more effective, more efficient and less costly.

As a result, I received regular calls from the media asking for interviews and quotes in articles they were writing. How did this happen? They found interesting content I published online. It is not that I've done anything exceptional, although I am consistent and take time to think about and write new content. I am sharing this with you because you can do it, too.

In the early 1990s, when web-based marketing was in its infancy, my team ignored the old rules and began to publish and post content. Many people told us we were giving people too much information, why even our competitors could read it! Gratefully, we published lots of content from a company magazine to regular web casts. Companies we never heard of, from places we never thought of, found us through search engines and contacted us for business opportunities. Understandably, online presence is a critical part of our marketing strategy.

Blogging

Develop and manage a blog strategy. Blogs are nothing more than short or long form interactive communication on the web. You can host one within your own site or let it stand alone on the Internet. Blogs do not require high-end design. Indeed, there are excellent WordPress templates that require very little effort to launch.

Blogging enables you to get your ideas out, attract interest, and generate response posts from others. A blog gives you a communication podium to build your reputation as an authority in your field and gain visibility for your company. Blogs allow you to push ideas into the marketplace as you think of them, generating instant feedback. You need a strategy for starting a blog—what do you want to say, to whom, and why? Above all, establish realistic goals and objectives to help your blog succeed.

With the power of search engines, your blog can be a vital and effective way for people to find you. Every word of every post is indexed by Google,

Yahoo!, LinkedIn, Facebook and other search engines, so when people look for information on the topics you write about, they find you. Often, your blog will help journalists find you. You may be quoted in newspapers and magazine articles without you the need to pitch a story.

Audio and Video

YouTube and iTunes are excellent ways to communicate complex subjects on the web. Your potential clients can see and hear you and gain an initial impression of you, your team and your company. Compact, visual and engaging, these tools are worth your investment in time and content, and are certain to enhance the visitor experience. Most websites are corporate brochures with no personality. Don't acquiesce to mediocrity for failure to do what is right in front of you.

LinkedIn

LinkedIn for networking is a compelling channel for marketing. In my 30 years in business, it is one of the most exciting tools I have found. When someone Googles your name, what do you think shows up in the top ten in your search? Your LinkedIn profile. Who developed and posted that profile? Of course, you did. What a great way to get your profile out and control your message. Here are some useful tips to turn LinkedIn into a powerhouse networking tool:

Upgrade your free membership to a Business subscription. The $25 monthly fee will provide you with additional networking tools that are immensely helpful:

- *Access to InMail.* A productive way to network with professionals outside of your network with whom you have no current connection or shared group. When you email, they can immediately check you out and review your profile.
- *Priority search results.* When other LinkedIn members conduct searches, your profile appears first in their results list, no matter how they sort results; that is, if a search is conducted, and results are sorted by degrees away, even if you are farther away than

someone else, you appear at the top of the list. This works like sponsored searches in Google and other search engines.

- *More search results.* The free membership provides 100 results per search; the Business membership provides 300 results per search.
- *Additional profile views.* Business membership allows you to see all the people who have viewed your profile.
- *Access to OpenLink network.* This is an extra way for people to find you, and for you to find networking contacts.

Spend some quality time updating/creating your profile.

- Pull key points from your resume or bio, but do not include the entire document on your LinkedIn profile. Generate only enough interest to encourage people to find out more about you.
- Add keywords to your profile to ensure more people find you in a targeted search.
- Add a professional-looking photo to your profile for a higher "sticky" factor. People like to put a face with a name.
- Include links to your profile on other professional networking sites such as Plaxo, Naymz and JobFox.
- Add your company's website to allow people to dig deeper.

Maximize your connections.

- Search former companies and school(s) for potential connections. Invite former colleagues and schoolmates to join your network, even if you might not know them personally. I've found that people, especially from my college, are very willing to network, simply because of the common factor of attending the same school.
- Invite friends and family to join your network. While I personally would not use a social networking space like Facebook for professional networking, I certainly use friends and family connections via LinkedIn for networking.
- Find new connections by importing your email address book contacts. LinkedIn makes this very easy to do. Also, check the

"people you may know" area for other potential connections, based on mutual connections, groups, or companies.

- When inviting new connections, always write a personalized note along with your invitation. If it is someone you do not know, or know well, specify how you found them, or how you are connected. Personalizing the note brings you much closer. I have found people who are three degrees away and connected with a note that mentions we have a contact in common.

Join LinkedIn groups.

- LinkedIn offers many user groups. Some require approval to join; as long as your experience is relevant, your request will be approved. Some types of groups:
  › School alumni (colleges, graduate schools, high schools you've attended)
  › Company alumni (companies where you've worked)
  › Industry interests (financial services, life sciences)
  › Geographic (San Diego business)
  › Functional (marketing, sales, finance)
  › Associations (NACD, Compensation and Benefit Groups, CPAs)
- Invite the moderator/creator of each group to your network.
- Browse group discussions frequently. Contribute often, but only if relevant. It's better to offer fewer posts that are highly relevant than many posts that are not.
- Find new contacts from group discussions. Read interesting topics, note interesting comments/answers. Invite those people to join your network. Include a note in your invitation indicating that you liked what he/she said on a topic in group discussion. This involvement shows interest and sparks future discussion.
- I am now posting articles on these group sites and can track how many people open them.

Get recommended.

- Ask everyone in your professional network to endorse you—former colleagues, schoolmates, professors, clients, vendors. No harm in asking, and I've found that most people willingly provide recommendations.
- Proactively recommend others in your network. Limit this to peers, direct reports, and schoolmates. Be selective in your choices of who to "proactively" recommend.
- Return the favor. When someone recommends you, provide a recommendation for them.
- Take a look at my page and see what people wrote.

Network for others. "What goes around comes around."

- If you come across an article of interest, a profile or piece of information that's relevant to a contact, a mutually beneficial group, or even a job posting, pass it along. Proactive networking on behalf of others will benefit you in return.
  - › **Example 1:** I am always on the "lookout" for anything to help my former colleagues who were laid off. They do not expect it, and leads are ALWAYS welcome. Put yourself on the receiving end of that relationship. Wouldn't you be pleased? These folks are likely to think of you when an interesting tidbit comes their way.
  - › **Example 2:** Keeping up with industry news and happenings is a great source for generating reasons to network. Find a great white paper? Send it along to a connection at a target company. It's one more connection point, one more way to keep you at the forefront of their mind.

Research. Research. Research.

- When you get a lead or a tip on a potential opportunity, or when you identify a new target company, search LinkedIn for second or third level connections to current or past employees. Use LinkedIn to get your foot in the door. I've found connections that are willing to hand-deliver my bio to the right person. These folks might also give you some insight into the company culture, or additional information on the situation.

- Company information on LinkedIn is quite valuable. Search for companies within your industry of interest. Gather company profile information for target companies. LinkedIn can provide information such as:
  › Popular/most viewed profiles
  › New hires
  › How you are connected to people at the company
  › How people at the company are connected to other companies
  › Where people worked before this company
  › Common job titles at the company
  › Gender breakdown (% male and % female)

Log In to LinkedIn. Every day.
- View updates from your network. Connections to new people, new group discussions and profile updates are all helpful.
- Check your profile statistics. Like traffic to your website, you need to know where you stand, who's interested and what you can improve.
- If you're looking for a job or want to help a key contact, then view the job board. I have this set as a module on my home page. It shows the three most recently posted jobs in my geographic area. On clicking, you will see all jobs posted. Some jobs (marked with a *) are only posted on LinkedIn. Add internal company recruiters to your network when possible.
- Update your status message frequently. Make it interesting, so that people will be intrigued by it. When you refresh or change your status, you will appear on the home page of the folks in your network. This keeps you "top of mind" in others.

Facebook

LinkedIn has been my preferred social media tool, however, at the time of this writing, I now find daily needs to do more on Facebook. David Meerman Scott in this book *The New Rules of Marketing & PR* opened my eyes to all social media.

According to Scott, *"people join Facebook groups because they want to stay informed, and they want to do it on their own time. Just as with blogs, the best way to maintain a Facebook group is simply to make valuable information available."*

With its power to connect, ability to create company fan pages and to set up a Facebook group, this medium is perhaps the fullest reverberation of the social web. Some have even described it as a springboard for revolution.

LEVERAGE MARKETING

Leverage marketing requires a great deal of patience, but the results are worth it. Comprised of several targeted campaigns at once, mostly through email (not spam), leverage marketing builds over time and creates growing brand awareness for your company name and offer. Some of my best clients came from this initiative.

The Internet is the greatest direct mail medium of all time because it gives you a marketing channel to reach people normally not accessible, and at a low cost. Using the Internet to leverage your marketing effort is a powerful promotional strategy to reach virgin prospects who don't know they need you, as well as people who may be in the market for your products and services, but don't know you are the answer.

Leverage marketing is as much art as it is science. It requires experimentation to find what works best in your market. Yes, we use our systematic MERGE Process to get in our prospect's door, but how you build awareness before that first appointment may be different every time. With leverage marketing, you need many different oars in the water to ensure you reach the shore.

Busy prospects don't want to hear about your products or services. They will grant you access only if you can grab their interest or to get them to think about an issue that has been on their mind.

Begin by reviewing your various contacts in each company and what information is available to you on the Internet or from public sources. Zero in on your prospect by finding out the answer to one or two key questions. If you are initiating the process—let's say the prospect organization has yet to begin a formal search for what you're offering—then ask *who has the level of authority to say yes to my offer?* If the company has already started a search, ask *who is in charge of the project?* In both cases, you are better off going in too high than too low.

Starting out too high typically results in a referral downward. It is a mistake to automatically begin your process at or near the top. You must stay within the general realm in which your prospect is likely to work. Never start out more than two or at the most three levels above where you think the ultimate decision maker is likely to reside. Please note that if you receive a referral directly to the top person, proceed full stop. My comments are limited to situations where you do not have a high-level referral.

In a simple but carefully orchestrated move, you are about to create enormous amounts of leverage that will quickly and effectively activate your prospects' bosses, causing them to take you and your offer seriously, and thereby increasing the probability of their granting you access.

Make your initial move by sending an email. I prefer email over regular mail if you can get access to the prospect address, which is usually easy to do. To activate your prospects' bosses, however, do not write your usual email or letter. Instead, your initial communication must include all of the following, more or less in the following order:

1. Send your email to your contact person; copy others in your prospect's organization. Everyone receives the exact same communication. By sending the email to one or two people in the company above your contact, you apply a little pressure to return your call or at least click respond and email you back.

This action is your primary tool for building leverage. The fact that you are letting your prospect know who else you've drawn in adds to your leverage. If the message and offering is attractive, you'll get some great results from this approach.

2. Next, you need to let the recipients know you understand their business and industry and have information that could prove helpful. List competitors or peers with whom you currently do business or that you plan to meet in the future.

   This strategy adds more external leverage because companies welcome an opportunity to benchmark against a peer group. Early in the email, I personalize the message to avoid the impression of spam: "I reviewed your public information and believe you will find value in a study we've completed on your peers."

3. All good marketing is about the offer. In the next step, you ask permission to give something of value and to keep the communication lines open. For example, by offering any of the documents below, you create incentives to respond:
   • An industry study
   • A peer analysis
   • A tailored solution to an ongoing problem
   • An invitation to an event

   Unfortunately many salespeople never get their foot in the door because they're not focused on what is important to their prospect; they are too focused on product features and benefits.

4. Next, ask the recipient's help to identify the most appropriate person (or group) within his organization to forward on your information. Put it at the beginning of the email to catch speed readers. Even if you know, ask anyway, because you want to create involvement and interaction among the email recipients to

continue to leverage contact. Even if they disagree on the most appropriate person or group for you, the interaction is exactly what you want. Simply ask, "Who is the appropriate person to send this information to?"

5. Give a very brief description of the value you offer and the action you want the person to take. Be concise and to the point. Some of my best campaigns offer a new report or white paper discussing a sensitive issue in their industry. I might say, "We have just completed a study on executive compensation and benefits that includes many of your peers." If I can point to something in the data that shows the impact on their company, all the better. The next action is "Would you like a free copy of the report?" I'm looking for a yes to kickoff the relationship.

Typically, the first action the recipient takes is to request the report. Now you have an opportunity to continue communication and start the educational process on the very topic he or she helped identify. Since the prospect has responded, your continued communication gets a little easier. Your follow-up messages can focus on the solution and ways you can help the situation. With this powerful, open dialogue established, you are well on your way to that all-important initial meeting. And each time you exchange emails, you build rapport and confidence in the next steps.

As discussed in the research chapter, gather ample information on the company and the individual prospect, learning the personal side, as well. If I know she attended the same school or her favorite football team had a recent victory, I'll note in the P.S. "Congratulations on a great win last weekend over USC." Here are a couple of examples of rapport-building via email. Initial email using a study as the incentive:

From: William MacDonald [mailto:bill@pastrategy.com]
Sent: Thursday, April 08, 2010 5:17 PM
To: Thornton, Leslie R.
CC: Jones, Robert R.
Subject: Study

We are in the process of completing a study on nonqualified executive benefits for companies in your peer group. Would you have interest in receiving a free copy of our findings?

If so, can I ask you to answer a couple of questions to clarify information? This information will be held confidential and only used in the broad study. The focus of the study will be on the design, funding and administration of your nonqualified deferred compensation plan and how it has impacted your overall corporate objectives.

Here is the list of the companies we will study:

Abercrombie & Fitch	Aéropostale
American Eagle Outfitters	AnnTaylor
Arcadia	Babies "R" Us
Benetton	Calvin Klein
The Children's Place	Dillard's
Express LLC	Fast Retailing
Foot Locker	Fruit of the Loom
Guess?	Gymboree
H&M	HSN
Inditex	J. Crew
J. C. Penney	Juicy Couture
Kohl's	L.L. Bean
Lands' End	Levi Strauss
Macy's	Marks & Spencer
Nautica Apparel	NIKE
Nordstrom	OshKosh B'Gosh
Phillips-Van Heusen	Polo Ralph Lauren
REI	Reebok
Retail Brand Alliance	Ross Stores
Saks	Sears
Talbots	Target
The Gap	TJX Companies
Tommy Hilfiger	VF
Wal-Mart	

William L. MacDonald
Chairman, President, & CEO
Pleine Aire Strategies, LLC
Phone: 213.598.7400
bill@pastrategy.com

Below are their responses (we changed the names to protect their information, but these are real responses). Notice that she passed the email on to the person in the organization she believed most appropriate. Leslie is her boss. I copied Robert Jones because Leslie reports up to him through one other person. This email generated 50 percent response from the companies we contacted:

> **From:** Smith, Ann [mailto:ASmith@abc.com]
> **Sent:** Monday, April 26, 2010 10:46 AM
> **To:** William MacDonald
> **Subject:** FW: study
>
> Hi, William.
> Leslie forwarded your email and asked me to touch base to see if we might be interested in participating in your study if there is still opportunity to do so. Can you give me a general idea of the sort of data you are expecting to include in the study results?
>
> Thanks!
> Ann Smith
> Vice President Compensation & Benefits

This initial response starts the dialogue going. Now, I am reaching out and asking for answers to important questions. Notice how freely the information flows, when the incentive (to get peer information) is strong. She also called this an "opportunity." I then sent her the questions, and she replied, keeping the dialogue moving. See her next response.

> **From:** Smith, Ann [mailto:Ann.Smith@abc.com]
> **Sent:** Thursday, April 29, 2010 9:53 AM
> **To:** William MacDonald
> **Subject:** RE: study
>
> Hi, William.
> Please see below for our answers. Thanks!
> Ann
> _____

From: William MacDonald [mailto:bill@pastrategy.com]
Sent: Thursday, April 29, 2010 7:17 AM
To: Smith, Ann
Subject: RE: study

We are finishing up the study, and have a couple of questions.
1.   How are you funding your current plan? (mutual funds, insurance)
     COLI
2.   Do you offer a rabbi trust?
     Yes
3.   Does the plan offer short term distribution payouts?
     If you mean in-service distributions, yes
4.   Who is the plan administrator?
     ABC is the Plan Administrator
5.   Has participation increased or decreased in 2009 over 2008?
     We saw a slight decrease in participation
6.   Does the company plan on reviewing its plan in 2010 or 2011?
     *We generally review the plan on an ongoing basis and do a more
     in-depth review approximately every 2-4 years*
7.   What was the objective of implementing the plan in the first place,
     and is it still meeting those objectives?
     To attract and retain people. Not sure, would like to discuss.

Here is another response from the same campaign. When you position
your message well and offer something of value, you will get great results.

From: Jessica Carter@XYZ.com [mailto:JCarter@XYZ.com]
Sent: Tuesday, April 20, 2010 11:10 AM
To: William MacDonald
Subject: FW: study

Hi William,
We would be happy to discuss our Benefit plans & receive a copy of the
findings; feel free to reach out to me.
Thanks, Jessica
Jessica Carter
Director-Compensation & Benefits
XYZ
Ph: 412-432-4539
Fax: 724-779-5742

White papers and studies that include valuable data make this strategy work.

As discussed earlier, one offering is to invite prospects to an event regarded as valuable. One of my directors, Dr. Arthur Laffer, the father of supply-side economics, is involved with our firm. As you know, he was also Economic Advisor to President Ronald Reagan.

While you may not have access to a Dr. Laffer (it is our good fortune), you can reach out to experts in a number of areas and position them as a drawing card. Consider an economics professor at a local university, reach out to a speaker's network, or find a business leader with a great message to share. Here is an example of the message I send inviting them to an event:

> **From:** William MacDonald [mailto:bill@pastrategy.com]
> **Sent:** Thursday, January 21, 2010 6:49 AM
> **To:** steve@chicagobancorp.com
> **Subject:** Lunch with Dr. Laffer
>
> I will be hosting a dinner with Dr. Arthur B. Laffer in Chicago on February 24th. The dinner will be for a small group (15 people), and we would like to have you join us. Will you be in town?
>
> As you know, Dr. Laffer is "The Father of Supply-Side Economics" (Laffer Curve), and was President Reagan's Economic Advisor. He is also Vice Chairman and a director of our organization, RCG.
>
> The dinner will be held at The Chicago Club at 81 East Van Buren Street. We'll meet at 6 p.m. for cocktails and begin dinner at 7 p.m. It should be a fun evening. Dr. Laffer will give us some insight on the economy and some stories of his days in the White House. Can you join us?
>
> William L. MacDonald
> Chairman, President, & CEO
> Pleine Aire Strategies, LLC
> Phone: 213.598.7400
> bill@pastrategy.com

Read his message below. You might imagine we've known each other for years. The funny thing is I have never met him before.

From: Steve Clark [mailto:steve@chicagobancorp.com]
Sent: Thursday, January 21, 2010 6:28 AM
To: William MacDonald
Subject: RE: Lunch with Dr. Laffer

Hi Bill,
I would be delighted to attend. See you at the club on the 24th.

Steve Clark
Stephen M. Clark
Chairman and Chief Executive Officer
Chicago Bancorp

If I had cold called Steve Clark, and asked to come in to see him, he would have said, "See Bob Smith my director of human resources, he handles things like you are discussing." This insider approach is a great way to step up higher in the organization. And you do not sell anything on the initial contact. In fact, at the dinner we do not discuss our organization. If it comes up in conversation, we respond only briefly. I use my research tools to build my list. Since Dr. Laffer was a professor at the University of Chicago and University of Southern California, I look for key prospects that hold senior positions, and could have been in his classes. It is amazing; people covet these opportunities. I once had a CFO of a $6 billion public company drive from Memphis to Nashville to attend a dinner. So if you use a well-known economist, look to her school for prospect building.

Our post-dinner strategy is to have a solid, well-thought-out follow-up. I usually ask Dr. Laffer to send his own personal letter, and then I send one with a gift (either one of Dr. Laffer's books, or a set of presidential cufflinks). I then ask for permission to meet by saying something like, "at our dinner, we did not discuss what our firm does, or the value we believe we can bring to your organization. I have done a lot of research on Chicago Bancorp and its peers, and would like to schedule a time to come out and discuss how we can help you attract, retain and reward the key people who make a difference."

My closing ratio for that initial meeting is 100 percent. To be sure, you really need to do your homework so you don't blow the opportunity.

Ideally, the prospect will ask others in his organization to join the meeting, a valuable step forward. Make sure you prepare well.

Even when people respond who can't attend the event, it opens the door for further communications. Follow up and let them know you will keep them in mind, or follow up and politely express your disappointment because you wanted to share your research. Believe me, it is sincere and it opens communications.

We use golf as another one of those events. Pick a great local course where people like to play (the more exclusive the better) and invite them to join you. Put together two or three foursomes; it works the same way as the dinners, especially for true golfers. It is a hole-in-one. You might involve a local celebrity to attract people, too. I am blessed to have Ernie Banks, the Chicago Cubs Hall of Famer, as a close friend. Again, a respected or beloved local celebrity works equally well. Put a good client in the same foursome with two or three prospects, and your client does the selling for you.

INDIRECT PROMOTION

If you can harness the power of third party endorsements, you add a reliable weapon to your marketing arsenal. This form of indirect promotion is a credibility builder and a cost-effective method to increase the visibility of your firm. When existing clients, industry experts, or the media communicate your message, albeit indirectly, you influence what others think and do. Let's zero in on a few forms that work well.

Press and Publicity

Place articles or offer an expert quote to the media. For instance, if you write an article for a trade magazine, it carries more weight than if you simply placed it in your newsletter. This effort helps to position you as a thought leader. A quote in the *Wall Street Journal* or *Business Week* sets you and your firm up as an expert. The media never calls this an implied endorsement, but in the eyes of readers, it does give a halo effect generated by the editorial reputation of the media outlet.

It is easier to get quoted or published than you may think. Begin by developing a contact list of all the reporters who cover your area of expertise. Do this organically by reading the mastheads of magazines or researching contacts on media websites. Or subscribe to services that generate the lists automatically. Some that come to mind are MarketWire or Business Wire. Be sure to send editors story ideas, reports and data. If you are known as an expert, and you are front and center in their contact file, they will call. If you build the reputation, they will come.

Another way to get the word out is a steady stream of newsworthy press releases on new products, services, promotions, staffing, awards, or expanded offices. Post these news announcements in your groups on LinkedIn and on your website. If you publish reports and studies, get the word out through press releases. They will end up on the web and be picked up in Google searches. Set a goal to put one out each month.

Public Relations

Many firms do not avail themselves of the power of PR. Either they do not understand it, believe it is too costly to hire a firm, or simply do not wish to invest the time. That is a regrettable stance because public relations, or PR, is one of the most cost-effective disciplines in the marketing universe. We've already covered one aspect above, working with the media to gain publicity. However, PR expands far beyond the press.

It is simple to develop your PR machine. Begin by attending trade shows and networking with like-minded professionals. When the time is right, exhibit with your own booth and staff. Send out advance invitations to clients and prospects to drop by. Be sure to create a hook that will pull qualified prospects into your exhibit. A drawing, a live performance, or a book signing can attract the right traffic. Find a way to get invited onto a panel workshop or as a speaker on the main agenda. Host a hospitality suite during the event.

Next, build a speaker's agenda for yourself by researching the best forums where you can deliver a good keynote speech.

There are dozens of local and national venues in your field that search for interesting speakers and new topics. In my case, I try to speak regularly at the National Association of Corporate Directors, Financial Executives International, Vistage, and Young Presidents' Organization. Think outside the box. You never know where you might meet your next big client.

Advisory Boards

One excellent way to promote your company in a highly professional way is to implement an Advisory Board. By its very presence, an Advisory Board helps your marketing effort because you associate with valuable collaborators on whom to test your business model and growth strategy. There are five important areas to focus on when setting up your board:

1. **Objective:** Make sure you have clear objectives and the members understand what is expected from them. Your board serves in an advisory capacity to target a portion of your business or help you formulate strategy. If you want their marketing help, let them know up front so there are no surprises.

2. **Select the Right People:** Diversify the composition of your board—a lawyer, accountant, professor, marketing leader, or banker, for example. These influencers should be current and active in their fields. A retired professional who still sits on corporate boards is ideal, but an inactive former head of a law or accounting firm is only valuable for his first two years in retirement. Remember, you want quick-study, critical thinkers. Surprisingly, you can attract excellent candidates at a reasonable cost. More on compensation later.

3. **Stay Focused; Keep Members Informed:** An Advisory Board is a superb asset; treat it as such. If a member makes an introduction to a coveted prospect, follow up with the member on your success or failure. Ensure that your Board is continuously thinking about your firm. Meet face-to-face at least four times per year, develop crisp, actionable meeting agendas, and intersperse these meetings with monthly conference calls. Invite your Advisory Board to your annual meeting, include spouses, and make the group part of your business family. They will enjoy

being part of a fast-growing organization where they can make a difference.

4. **Set Expectations:** As we discussed above, make sure they understand their role and what is expected. If the board is there for marketing, don't hide behind another topic. Be up front; these are big boys and they will know how the game is played.

5. **Compensation:** Board member compensation can be made in several ways. You need to pay the member for his involvement and time. A percentage fee of the transaction may be prohibited by certain industries. Suggestions:

   • Meeting fees. Pay an annual retainer such as $5,000 or $2,500 per quarter. You could also pay a profit-sharing bonus at year-end.

   • Pay per prospect meeting. If the member lines up a high-level meeting, pay $250 to $500 per success with either shares of stock in your company or an annual profit payment.

   • Give your member something special. Consider buying hours in a fractional jet service; award them with hours. Or you could provide medical insurance or other benefits.

   • Stock in the company and a small fee.

Be sure to promote your Advisory Board everywhere possible. Issue a press release announcing formation; list their profiles on your website and in your corporate brochure; refer to the Board often in your presentations, consulting conversations, and networking. An Advisory Board is a major asset. Leverage it. Few firms, if any, can afford not to have an Advisory Board.

Paid Advertising

Paid advertising, whether print, electronic or digital, is an expensive proposition. However, it is an effective way to broadcast to multiple prospect groups, control your message, and deliver a strong call to action.

Unless you represent a large organization with supersized budgets, national print advertising, television or radio is usually off limits to most companies because of up front production costs, rotating media buys and costs-per-impression. You may be able to afford smaller local markets but in general, advertising for professional service firms does not deliver the return on investment required.

Over the years, I have implemented ad campaigns in two ways: one-way communications (radio, television, newspapers, magazine), and two-way with instantaneous response. Success came with two-way instantaneous response via phone or email.

Whatever you do, always offer something of value in your ad. You want the reader, viewer or listener to engage in direct response. Offer a study, white paper, or useful report. Always post your URL and, if appropriate, a direct phone or email contact in every ad to drive traffic to your site. The ad must drive prospects back to you to ask for something of value.

There you have it: your promotional plan. Marketing education; online presence; leverage marketing; indirect promotion; advisory boards; and paid advertising. Think of it as your six-pointed star to light your way to profits.

As Peter Drucker maintained, "Business only has two functions. Marketing and innovation. Marketing and innovation make money. Everything else is a cost." Invest in marketing if you want to be profitable. Because if you are not marketing, only one of two outcomes occurs—your business either stagnates or shrinks.

8 | A Measure of Trust

What Matters Most

The reasons people buy complex intangibles are a messy blend of mental gymnastics and unexpressed feelings. We humans are made up of two distinct but equal parts: One is rational; the other irrational. This paradox is blindingly apparent in the decision to buy or not to buy professional or financial services.

I was always trained that people buy on emotion and justify on logic. "The sale is emotionally driven and emotionally decided. Then it is justified logically," confirms best-selling sales author Jeffrey Gitomer.

Being the left-brained person I am, I tested this buy-on-emotion-justify-on-logic belief hundreds of times in my career, with some surprising revelations. In one case, the senior executive of a major corporation accepted my verbally delivered solution on the spot, without ever receiving a written proposal—an engagement that became quite valuable financially.

In another opportunity, the prospect opened up his entire management team to us for internal interview and review without a signed contract. Now, I am not a miracle worker, and I did have to perform well, but these prospects accelerated the process because they knew I listened, engaged, demonstrated an authentic concern from day one. And I solved their problem with a clear process that led to the result desired.

The development of trust is often attributed to chemistry, intuition, gut feeling, perception or some other hard-to-explain phenomenon. In the golden age of television, Johnny Carson and Ed McMahon hosted a popular game show called *Who Do You Trust?* Couples had to take a leap of faith and trust each other to come up with the right answer to Johnny's quizzing. In one burst of hilarity after another, America saw the limits of trust.

Trust is a leap of faith. In my experience, most salespeople and some consultants either do not know or fear to ask what prompts a prospect to trust or distrust their interaction. At some level, we don't want to know our twitch is bothersome, our speech is irritating or we're not that likeable. This said, what is trust and how do you cultivate it?

LITMUS TEST

Are you willing to recommend a key competitor to an important client, if you are unable to solve that client's problem? Think long and hard about this question. If you are unwilling, it is fair to say your own interests take precedence over your prospect's or client's interests. This one question can separate the trustworthy from the self absorbed. Understandably, you don't want to walk away from business, let alone plant it in the hands of a competitor. But that is exactly what you must do. Your prospect wants to experience genuine trust that you care about his success. He needs your solution; he wants the feeling of trust.

Whenever I become overly invested in landing the sale, I stop and check my ego at the door, and ask myself three clarifying questions: What's the right thing to do here? What's best for the long-term well-being of my client? How do I create real and lasting value in the relationship?

What I've learned is that clients will instinctively trust you when you:
- Convey genuine concern for their outcomes
- Communicate clearly and consistently
- Demonstrate professional integrity without compromise
- Show courage in the clinches and accountability across the relationship

Of course, it is essential to be good at what you do, but you have probably also noticed that few salespeople outright fail in this business because they lack product knowledge. Service providers and the entire vendor community flood their sales channels with high quality information. When a sales professional does fail, it is usually because she fails to build high-trust client relationships, which is the only sure-footed path to repeat business and referrals.

Trust is the single most important prerequisite for a great client relationship, one that produces bookable results with less time and effort. And you can't teach trustworthiness, in the same way that character is next to impossible to teach. Trust emerges with a decision, a choice, and a judgment that resides deep within each of us. And it expresses itself in daily behavior.

When prospects do not respond to your advice, when they do not open up and tell you their financial truths or worries, it is because they do not trust you—not enough to move forward. If a prospect shuts down your solution, he does not believe you have his best interest at heart. While it is not easy to recover from a trust deficit, it is not impossible.

TRUST FORGIVES MISTAKES

In a recent client assignment with a Fortune 500 company, my team and I worked through our process to design a unique funding approach for our client's deferred compensation plan. As we normally do, we assembled a team from the client side to discuss the issues and review alternatives, some of which we did not offer.

As a collaborative group, we crafted a complex strategy that allows a deferred compensation participant to take the funding vehicle (in this case insurance) with him as an asset in the event of a departure. This strategy provides the participant with benefit security as well as control of a tax-advantaged asset—exactly what the client wanted.

Our firm had installed similar strategies with two other clients and had vetted the process with our legal counsel and the client's accountants. If the transfer took place with a gain, there was one adverse tax consequence.

Sparing you the details, the result was not advantageous for younger executives, which we knew. However, the two previous clients implemented the strategy for older executives, and it worked well.

During the engagement, we expanded the group of participants and continued to model the assumptions based on the older individuals. For reasons I simply cannot explain, we overlooked this tax consequence, which impacted 30 percent of the group and would have added cost.

As we began to interact with outside advisors, the client's law firm brought the potential issue to the table. I could have died. We knew better. In fact, we had legal opinions in our research files. I immediately feared that the entire client team had lost trust in us. I personally felt they might have thought we were hiding something. It was an awful embarrassment.

Quickly, I called the treasurer to apologize and explain our oversight, as well as to reassure him that we are thorough in our process and do not usually make these types of mistakes. We had spent the last four months working very closely with their team and diving into all of the numbers and issues on this topic, only to miss this one. Without hesitation, he said, "We know it was an oversight. We all should have picked up on it sooner, so let's focus on how we can make this work now that we have this issue to deal with."

His comments speak to the collaborative process with our team, and his experience of teamwork with us. We marched forward and continued to prepare for the presentation for the board. While we lost a few months, trust was never an issue.

Trust is, however, a major issue in business today. Everywhere we look, there are trust deficits between the American public and our financial, political and educational institutions. Not all, but enough that the national psyche is steeped in skepticism, and the public trust is at its lowest. Arguably, legislative reforms may help; however, trust still comes down to a personal experience between two people with open minds.

RISE OF FIDUCIARIES

Under the Dodd-Frank Bill, *Restoring American Financial Stability Act of 2010*, a concerted effort is being made to reset the rules of engagement for consumers, investors and financial entities and their agents. I understand the original bill is designed to promote the financial stability of the United States by improving accountability and transparency in the financial system; to end "too big to fail;" to protect the American taxpayer by ending bailouts; and to protect consumers from abusive financial services practices.

The investor protection portion of this financial reform bill intrigues me most. Regulators now have authority to require all financial advisors to act in their clients' best interest by disclosing fees, disciplinary actions, conflicts of interest and commissions paid on transaction.

It is noteworthy that the "abusive financial services practices" of the few have compelled the many to come to terms with the issue of trust. Transparency is intrinsic to trust.

One might say this bill is long overdue or a knee-jerk reaction to a posse of scoundrels who misappropriated other people's money because they were greedy and clearly not mindful of the client's best interest. In the qualified plan business, ERISA spells out and demands fiduciary responsibility or plan participants have a right to sue. And they do. Case law is full of thorny and colorful examples. Put simply, fiduciary is synonymous with trust.

According to Matthew D. Hutcheson, MS, CPC, AIFA™, CRC®, an independent professional fiduciary and a nationally recognized authority on qualified plans and fiduciary responsibility, the fiduciary standard of care rests on one's ability to:

- Put the plan participants' best interests first
- Act with the prudence, skill, care, diligence and good judgment of a professional
- Not mislead sponsors or participants and disclose all material facts
- Avoid conflicts of interest and fully disclose and fairly manage

Straightforward. No mystery. And it should be applicable to anyone who does any type of financial services business. Keeping advisors or consultants in legal compliance is fodder for another book. Let's assume you seek to be trustworthy, not because the law says so, but because it is the only way of business that makes sense.

What can you do to help frame the perception of behavior and deliver an experience of trust, even before it is instilled in the client mind? In a word, process. The MERGE Process.

INVITING TRUST

Throughout this book, we write about development of process in research, strategy, solutions, communication and marketing. Process is especially essential to selling complex intangibles. It invites trust by reducing the unexpected. It allows clients to experience structure and direction with a sense of control. It gives you the capability to manage expectations and make it easier for clients to reach winning decisions without buyer remorse.

Professionals who build client relationships on process-driven trust are often asked to take on the complete menu of client financial needs. And clients are more likely to buy without feeling "sold." Without the presence of trust, particularly in financial or professional services, no meaningful business can emerge. When you are trusted, you do not need to rely on sales tactics, objection scenarios or elaborate closing techniques.

Know your prospect inside and out. Understand his problem. Understand your value. Craft a well-considered solution. Follow your process. And show you care.

Trust will emerge like beams of light through a dark forest.

9 INKING THE DEAL

The Engagement Letter

"You're hired." Welcome words to a consultant. Now you can engage your process and help your client solve his problem or issues. To ink the deal, however, it is wise to commit to writing everything that was discussed and agreed upon to this point. Enter the Engagement Letter.

Some call an engagement letter the proposal, agreement, contract, or scope of work. Semantics aside, I prefer the engagement letter because, in essence, you do engage the client in a mutuality of purpose. Also, any whiff of the word contract can put clients off. Engagement Letter or Letter of Agreement works well.

A word of warning: Do not risk verbal agreements, even though they can be perfectly valid and binding in a court of law. Put your agreement in a formal engagement letter to define performance on both sides and to prevent misunderstandings when memory or attention fades. Besides, once the client sees the letter, it can break the log jam of indecision. The authors of *Marketing for Financial Advisors* aptly call this condition "psychological inertia," that all-too-human tendency to put things off.

WHY DO CLIENTS ASK FOR PROPOSALS?

I asked a dozen of our existing clients this question and directed my question to the head of human resources of mid-size to large organizations.

Here are typical responses:

> *"It's our company policy to look at more than one vendor."*
> *"We need the proposal to make an informed decision."*
> *"Proposals help to clarify some of the complex information discussed by all of the vendors."*
> *"We use the proposal to slow down the sales process so we can be more objective and make an informed decision."*
> *"To solicit ideas and become educated on certain topics."*

Clients always ask consultants or advisors for proposals or quotations to determine if everyone is on the same page, as well as to frame their final decision. And remember, there are many people in your business calling on the same prospects.

The engagement letter enables the prospect to compare vendors, products and prices, as well as clear up conflicting information. With complex sales, there are multiple decision makers. Your engagement letter may be read by someone who influences the decision that you will not meet. Their only impression of you and your firm is the engagement letter.

Your engagement letter must contain a compelling business case for your understanding of the challenge or problem, and your recommendation on solutions. If you follow the MERGE Process, preparing the engagement letter and proposal portion flows logically. You do your research. You probe for issues to help your client. You lay the groundwork for solutions by testing ideas and approaches during all your interactions. You are now ready to recommend the "engagement."

To get at the business case, ask these questions well before you craft the engagement letter:

> *"When you compare different vendors, what is the most important factor in choosing one over the other? The last time you made this kind of decision, what factors did you use to guide your decision?"*
> *"What did you look for? Did that work for you?"*

NOT ANOTHER PROPOSAL

In my experience, many consultants have difficulty putting together an engagement letter or proposal. Time, focus and resources are typically limited. In one bank environment, the relationship managers spent an average of eight to ten hours a week on business proposals. That gets old.

Too often, people cut and paste the same weary language from previous proposals, simply changing the names of the usual suspects. Have you ever forgotten to do that and sent the wrong proposal to the right prospect? Embarrassing. Another problem with proposal writing is too much detail. We think we need to cover every nook and cranny but trust me, prospects will not read it. If the proposal is too hefty, they won't even pick it up.

THE BASIC COMPONENTS

The main purpose of the engagement letter is to get hired, the flashpoint in the MERGE Process. Because I'd rather see you spend your time in service to the client than writing lengthy documents, let's simplify.

Here are some of the basic sections of an effective letter or proposal from the standpoint of someone who has read and written hundreds:

Executive Summary

Review your understanding of issues, concerns and problems. Use the prospect's language, especially if it was already cited in a Request for Proposal. Hint at a solution. Lay out your qualifications to offer the solution. Be optimistic but do not promise outcomes you cannot deliver. In general, keep your summary to half a page and the entire document to three to four pages maximum.

Define the Project

Be specific on objectives and requirements. Create a one or two sentence premise as your project definition, if possible. Measure everything you write against this premise to determine if the language complements or compromises the intended direction. Any debatable areas must be sourced with pristine research. Link your ideas to prospect needs. Discuss major assumptions, unknowns or obstacles to overcome.

Present the Solution

Present a clear idea and a focused plan to achieve your solution. Discuss methodology. Assure your reader with well-thought-out argument or rationale. Define success for the project. How will everyone know when the engagement has succeeded, by what measurements, what standards? Specify guidelines, deadlines, deliverables, staff assignments, resource allocations and, importantly, a detailed budget.

Next Steps

Tell your prospect what steps to take next. Is it as simple as "sign and return" the engagement letter, or do you need a follow-up meeting, another piece of data put into place? Be extremely clear about what action you wish taken next. Naturally, close with a genuine statement of anticipation of success.

Above all, follow a logical sequence with consistent organization. Make your engagement letter easy to skim by using strong subheads and bullets to highlight your narrative. And allow for eye-relieving white space.

What to Avoid

- Boring, pro-forma language; be persuasive, interesting and readable
- Passive voice; use active verbs, simple construction and lively language
- Typos, grammatical errors, misspelled names or proper nouns
- Rambling to fill up space; keep it to the point
- Overuse of design, diagrams or visuals; find a pleasing balance
- Overkill, overpromising, unsupported statements
- Lecturing and subjectivity

BE PERSUASIVE

Most proposals I receive from vendors are unpersuasive. They launch into a long monologue with company superlatives and technical product details spilling off the pages. I can find the same information the vendor's website. The proposals do not focus on our business problems or the financial value I can expect from a business relationship. I have to dig through poorly written, jargon-stuffed narrative to find my answers.

The major killer? Misspellings, grammar and punctuation errors. More than half the vendors who present to our company misspell my name: McDonald, not MacDonald. Do you think I notice this? If the purpose of the engagement letter is to move the sales process along toward closure, why throw up needless roadblocks?

The actual decision maker for your project may never attend the meeting at which you propose the engagement. The engagement letter helps to level the playing field with other competitors and establishes your credibility. Years back, one of my clients asked me to review three proposals for property and casualty insurance on his building. I explained I didn't know much about the subject, but he said, "You know more than I do."

I scanned the three proposals and immediately eliminated one. Can you believe one of the firms wrote its proposal and pricing on a yellow legal pad? It focused only on the cost of coverage with no value-added. It was the cheapest, but I personally had no confidence in their firm. My first impression was drawn from that yellow legal pad.

The second proposal was the thinner of the two remaining. The third was 200-plus pages, but I would read it later for my client. The second proposal did an excellent job of demonstrating the firm understood the client's needs. It outlined both the current cost of premiums and the economic loss if the building burned down. The firm showed both replacement cost and other economic comparisons to help educate me on the topic. The proposal flowed well and followed a logical decision making process, with supporting arguments and credentials. If I had a claim, I would want this firm to oversee it.

The final proposal, I'll be honest, I never finished reading. It relied on copies of policies, lots of technical language, and 200 pages. Many pages were photocopied, none were numbered, and there was no organization. Of course, I was already influenced by the second proposal— direct, short and concise. This review was a valuable lesson for me.

I have since reviewed many proposals as further study. I surveyed International Forum members for copies of their proposals. Some were selling products, while a good number offered a fee-based process. A number of members confided in me that they were not landing a high percentage of the deals they proposed. It didn't surprise me. The majority of these proposals were highly technical and hard to follow, and I'm in the same business. Not one mentioned a value proposition or explained the financial impact of the process.

Share the Economics

Every proposal must show the economic impact your value proposition brings to the prospect. It is hard work, so we often avoid it. Address it by building a tight case study. Using case studies of similar situations could be helpful, too. Also find out what kind of outcome the key decision makers think is important for their company. In the initial face-to-face initial meeting, learn the answers to such defining questions as, "If we are engaged to do this project for you, what are three things you would hope to accomplish?" The answer is your premise in the proposal.

Take care to emphasize your differentiation and explain how your organization's competitive advantage is able to produce the results when others may not. Prospects, clients and customers want to know what makes you different from and better than your competition. More importantly, they want to know why those differences benefit their company.

Your Storyboard

We use a storyboard process for pulling information together for the engagement letter. The storyboard process was first developed at the Walt Disney

Studio during the early 1930s and is still used today by film, animation and design companies. The process graphically depicts the elements of the business story you wish to tell. The first step: Understand your intended message and how you want to communicate it. If you don't understand the message, no one will. Next, get all the facts up on a white board (your storyboard). Three questions will help. I learned this technique while serving in Vietnam, when I had to communicate back to base camp in a short and concise way. Ask yourself and your team: What do you know about the situation? What don't you know? What do you think?

Simple, yes, but also powerful in helping you think through what you need and what is missing. Many executives use an old sales tactic for proposal writing: *"Tell 'em what you're going to tell 'em, tell 'em, and then tell 'em what you told 'em."* Let's drill down on specifics beyond my basic sections cited earlier. A well-organized engagement letter covers:

1. An understanding of the client's needs
2. Key goals and objectives
3. Project scope and deliverables, showing economic value
4. Staffing
5. Timetable
6. Estimated project fees and expenses
7. Summary

UNDERSTANDING CLIENT NEEDS

Begin your proposal with the client need or problem, and be certain that there is agreement on this critical starting point. Follow the MERGE consulting process, your research and your probing to identify issues. Summarize the business situation and focus on the gap to be closed or the value to be added. In this way, you prove you listened and that your products or services will help them address their needs. Secure client agreement along the way, so that he asks for a proposal. Now you have the opportunity to offer an unsolicited proposal without facing any direct competition.

Key Goals and Objectives

Next, focus on client results by outlining the key goals and objectives, illustrating the benefits of your solution. Here, you make your recommendation, focus on pain and gain, and give the client a sense of return on investment (ROI). You might also consider briefly covering alternative solutions—not to recommend but rather to present why they are not as desirable as your solution. This approach allows you to dismiss competing alternatives and signals to the client that your firm is thorough.

Project Scope and Deliverables

In the next segment, demonstrate your capability, background and resources. Client references and case studies are an effective way to get the message across. Graphs, charts and photos help to bring visual impact to your message. Our firm relies on charts and graphical representations of information to communicate, especially when heavy use of numbers is required. We continually test what works and doesn't work. A good resource is the book *Say it With Charts* by Gene Zelazny.

Staffing

Outline staffing, who will lead the project, and who forms the team. Add short, well-written biographical paragraphs in the back of the engagement proposal, along with executive-style photos. A staffing narrative allows you to further differentiate. One of your team members may have direct industry experience, or perhaps you plan to use only senior people to manage the project, so emphasize that involvement.

Timetable

When dealing with major companies, take heed. They value organization, deadlines and timetables. Lay out the scope of the project and all key dates for certain action. Pay close attention to pacing items for both you and the client. I always use a timetable to manage the project cycle, beginning with the implementation date and working back to account for all actions.

Estimated Project Fees and Expenses

Be as clear as possible in delineating project fees and handling expenses. If you use a three or four step process, consider breaking down the fees in steps to help the client discuss value at any point in the project.

SUMMARY

Do not miss this golden opportunity to restate and summarize all the levels of value you bring to the project. Tie the entire document together at this point, making it easy for the reader to make a decision in your favor.

The good news—once the engagement letter is signed, you are in control. Writing proposals is hard work but worth the reward, as long as you write for qualified prospects only. Avoid playing the numbers game.

Remember my 10-5-3-1 formula? It works for a reason. Out of ten qualified prospects—where I have done my research—only five will be in a current position to consider an engagement letter now. The other five stay in the pipeline. Out of the five engagement letters issued, my team will be hired on three, a good batting average. If the timing isn't right or the prospects have not recognized the issues, do not invest time writing a quality proposal.

I credit our high closing ratio to effective engagement letters. Remember, the objective is to get hired and move the prospect into the consulting process, where he can make bite-size decisions each step of the way. The decision to hire you is a big step for him, but it still only involves a small fee and commitment of time.

Finally, there are many books on the subject of proposal and presentation writing. Some of the helpful books for me were *Persuasive Business Proposals* by Tom Sant and *Writing Winning Business Proposals* by Richard C. Freed, Shervin Freed and Joe Romano. With the help of my partner Bill Forrest, one of the best writers I know, our firm became known for high quality reports and presentations.

We learned early on that if our presentations and proposals were sloppy and disorganized, our audience might also assume our work was sloppy and disorganized. So it was important for us to apply the structure of our critical thinking to proposals and presentations. We developed an internal quality control group to nitpick the report and ensure perfection before it was sent out. And we always finalize reports and presentations, including printing, copying and binding, at least 24 hours prior to the meeting. That way your team has time to rehearse, role-play and plan for questions and answers.

Our clients make their decisions based on what they see, hear and sense in what they read; they want advisors who take their own work seriously. No doubt, your prospects do, too.

10 | ONCE THE SALE IS MADE
Stay Engaged

In his book *The Practice of Management*, Peter F. Drucker wrote, "There is only one valid definition of business purpose: to create a client." Now that we have created the client, as evidenced by your engagement letter, the most important work lies ahead. We must retain the relationship by staying engaged.

At this point, your client relationship should intensify and evolve into a lasting and profitable relationship, depending, of course, on the quality of your service and how well you and your team manage the relationship.

Richard Gerson, author of *Beyond Customer Service: Effective Programs for Retaining Your Customers*, claims "it costs five or six times more to get a new client versus retaining an existing one." He argues that you can calculate the value of lost business from that.

THE RIGHT CLIENT

V. Kumar's book *Managing Customers for Profit* examines customer acquisition cost in greater detail. To fully assess the cost, you need to understand Customer Lifetime Value. Kumar shares a number of interesting stories on organizations which focused totally on client retention and then went out of business because they acquired and retained the wrong clients. If you followed the MERGE Process, selected the right client, and brought value to the relationship through your collaborative process, it is my experience that the engaged step flows naturally.

MANAGE EXPECTATIONS

Build a strategy to manage your client's long-term expectations. All organizations have an opportunity to grow future profits by managing client relationships. A good example comes from an unlikely place. A number of years ago, colleague Eric Thibault and I were having dinner in a hotel restaurant when we looked over to the table next to us and saw Gene Simmons from the rock group KISS. The band had played in Kansas City the night before. Gene and the group were holding a strategic planning meeting over dinner. We overheard Gene ask the group, "What did we do right last night, and what can we do differently to give our fans a better experience?" Throughout dinner, they probed for ideas to improve KISS's customer service. A slew of vendors lined up every 15 or 20 minutes to pitch KISS on new products to sell at performances to increase revenues with concert-goers. It was impressive to watch the band members sort through the pitches and turn away products they felt would compromise the fan experience. This scenario is a great example of understanding your client and focusing on your value.

80:20 PROFITS

John J. Sviokla and Benson P. Shapiro explain in *Keeping Customers* that keeping good customers should be as natural to a business as breathing is to human beings. Yet many businesses are so oriented toward attracting new clients that they do not invest resources in sustaining long-term relationships after the sale is made.

That said, I have also found many firms do not consistently identify their most profitable clients; they lose out on countless opportunities to generate solid profits in the long term. I know it's a cliché—80-20 rules! Eighty percent of your profits come from the top 20 percent of your clients. Sviokla and Shapiro also point out that to keep profitable clients, sellers must recognize how the relationship evolves over time. The resources you allocate to client acquisition today may not be sufficient to support future sales.

The last step in the MERGE Process is to stay engaged, and it requires commitment and a focus on continually creating the greatest possible value to clients without sacrificing profits.

To build profitable relationships, stay focused on these six areas and your client will stay engaged:

1. Put the client first, and make it your number one focus.
2. See your value proposition through the client's eyes.
3. Focus on guarantees.
4. Continue to invest in your relationship.
5. Capitalize on client satisfaction and profit from it.
6. Develop a system to measure what matters.

CLIENT FIRST

One lesson I learned from Ben Shapiro is the client first principle. Your whole firm should be focused on your client's demands and concerns. You took your client through the MERGE Process, led with your value proposition and met client issues head on. As this client continues to grow, new issues will percolate up. If you don't pay close attention, those issues can drip right into a competitor's hands.

Look outside your firm. Focus on what is important to your client. Develop client service systems to evolve with client demands. Today's technology sets the expectation of near-instant response. In fact, consider benchmarking your firm to other providers or industries you hold in high regard. In all likelihood, these best practices firms walk the talk and do put clients first. Work diligently to emulate those with world-class service. And your clients will continually engage themselves.

Through Client Eyes

For any client relationship to survive, it is crucial to always see value through the client's eyes. Robert B. Miller and Stephen E. Heiman, authors of *Successful Large Account Management*, emphasize, "From a purely practical dollars and cents standpoint, you'd better see things as the people in your large accounts do, because the decisive factor in any sale is the clients' receptivity to what you're offering. That receptivity is inevitably a function of the way their companies, not yours, see the world."

Unfortunately, some firms are not organized to deliver on client expectations of value, especially post-sale. Firms erect barriers to client understanding, the unintended consequence of an internal, institutionalized focus. Get out of the office. Ride with salespeople. Ask clients what they think. Jettison any policies or procedures that restrict employees from doing the right thing for the client. That alone will become a powerful engagement magnet.

In each of my roles as CEO, I met as often as possible with clients. The dialogue was a great reality check. I would ask our clients, "Over the last two years I'm sure we did many things right, and some things wrong. What should we continue doing and what should we stop?" If I was in front of a coveted prospect, I'd always ask, "Who is your number one service provider? And what does the firm do for you that makes them number one?" My initial engagement strategy rested on that answer.

FOCUS ON GUARANTEES

In the consumer products business, product quality is communicated in part by a warranty. You buy a car, flat screen TV or a microwave oven, and the manufacture issues you a time-specific warranty to replace the item under certain conditions of defect. In the financial services business, no such guarantee exists. You'd be amazed if your estate plan came with a guaranteed lifetime review. Yet the assurance of a guarantee would presumably count most in financial or professional services. Ask the millions of people hurt by the financial meltdown of 2008.

Of course, services are hard to guarantee. They are delivered by humans, who are far less predictable than machines on shop floors or servers in IT centers. You can guarantee a camera because the consumer can inspect it before purchase and send it in for repair, if necessary. But how can you pre-inspect a financial plan, a will or a trust? Obviously, you can't. But you can guarantee high-quality customer service.

A guarantee isn't as scary as it may sound. Most consultants work under an implied guarantee anyway. With a legitimately unhappy client, a reputable consultant will fix the problem by doing additional work or reducing fees. In effect, you are making good on an implied guarantee. Why not offer it up front where it can benefit you and your client? If you're serious about service excellence and client results, put some teeth into your assertions.

A good guarantee is straightforward. David Maister, an authority on professional service firms, offers this guarantee on his website:

> "These fees are subject to an unconditional client satis-
> faction guarantee: If when the work is done, the client
> does not feel that full value was received, then the client
> decides how much it was worth and how much to pay
> (if anything)."

Nothing shuts down an overpromising consultant more quickly than the specter of a guarantee. With a guarantee in place, the consultant and client must reach precise agreement on project objectives, outcomes, and measurements of satisfaction. This level of rigor leads to a less ambiguous proposal, a more rational price, and better marching orders for those working on the project. Guarantees also elevate a firm's culture of service quality because its reputation and therefore, its financial well-being are on the line for every project.

Guarantees may not suit every consultant or client. If your service is mature and your delivery airtight, you may be able to absorb the added risk of guarantees. If not, multiple service failures could put you out of business. Also, some clients are not that interested in guarantees, especially if your service is already viewed as high quality or you work in a sector known for top-notch service.

My firm developed a "performance guarantee" and wrote service contracts with our clients for deferred compensation administration. We spelled out client expectations such as quarterly financial reports within three days of the close of a quarter. If that was important to the client, and we failed, we reduced or eliminated our fees.

INVEST IN RELATIONSHIPS

Client expectations continue to change, especially as new people join the client company. How many times have you lost clients when someone new takes over? Keep your contacts active. Always bring new ideas and concepts to their attention. I personally try to attend their company's activities, like their annual shareholders' meeting, and get involved with things that interest them, such as their charities. Too often, senior members of the service provider pass the service aspect on to a client service team, then disappear. What happens next is not pleasant. The relationship drifts down to the bottom layers in the company and gets buried in minutiae. Invest in a client relationship far more than in a prospect; they respond better to new ideas, and they generate more profit.

PROFIT FROM CLIENT SATISFACTION

Customarily, financial and professional service firms focus on revenues derived from fees or commissions. I focus on profits. By managing profitable sales yields, the results are far more satisfying. But it requires constant review of client behavior to estimate both value of service and the cost of providing that service to the client, as Sviokla and Shapiro point out in *Keeping Customers*.

In certain businesses, like retirement planning or health insurance, the long-term relationship is built around a service platform that manages hundreds, if not thousands, of employee and participant interactions. Many competitors give this service away on the front end to land the product sale. That's dangerous. You need to operate with full transparency and help educate the client on the true value and actual cost of this service. If you do not operate with full transparency, your firm may find itself providing more services for less money, a value proposition with diminishing return.

MEASURE WHAT MATTERS

To keep a client engaged after the sale requires you to put him first in all aspects of the relationship. It also requires that you know with some certainty if he continues to be pleased with your service, particularly with those services delivered by employees. This effort is daunting if you have a large organization because it is so difficult, if not impossible, to monitor the entire array of servicing activities occurring in your organization daily.

Short of checking everything yourself, you need to trust and verify with those on the frontlines, the client service team. Then you need to arm them with an effective measurement system that will paint a clear picture of the state of service in your company. It doesn't have to be complex. A monthly or quarterly phone questionnaire to a rotating list of clients can yield actionable information. If possible, create a continuous feedback loop by bringing together every point on the relationship path—sales channel, administration team, customer service people—and providing them with a simple and reliable mechanism to report client complaints, compliments or ideas.

However you decide to implement measurement, make the commitment. Develop a service profile of key performance indicators, quantitative metrics, and qualitative attitudes to reflect your desired standards of service, and measure regularly. It should include details of both client and employee service performance. Study such indicators as employee training tracked to client complaints, or client acquisition tracked to website conversion, or ratio of proposals to closed sales. Every business sector has its own unique set of measurements. Of course, be careful what you ask for. You may end up with a mound of data and no time to analyze it. Also, be sure to make room to change indicators as your business changes or evolves. Measurement is a dynamic process.

Above all, measure what the client values. Our organizations spent considerable time with clients up front to understand what services they most value. Then we matched performance measurements to what is valued and build out our employee incentive program to match the performance measurements. Though a small example, if a client needs its financial plan report within three days following a quarter, and we deliver in four, it is not acceptable. Do not be afraid to put your money where your service is and build a performance-based client service contract.

Staying engaged with a client is one part common sense and ten parts caring. Put her first, see through her eyes, offer a guarantee, invest in the relationship, and measure everything you can. I am reminded of a classic statistic reported by the Office of Technology Assessment years back:

For every one client that takes the time to complain, there are nine others who simply walk away, never say a word, and give their business to a competitor.

Celebrate the one by measuring the many.

A Parting Thought

Financial services and professional services are painfully complex fields. Life is short, so break ranks with conventional wisdom. Steer clear of complexity.

If you grin from ear to ear at the sound of the words, "You are hired, when can we start?" as often as we do, I urge you to embrace simplicity. Adopt the common sense simplicity of our MERGE Process, or adapt portions of it to fit your consulting style and situation. I promise, it will create trust in prospects and clients and energy for your business, and put a prosperous smile across your face.

ABOUT THE AUTHOR

William L. MacDonald is the Founding
Partner of several leading organizations in
the executive compensation and benefit
consulting field, notably Compensation
Resources Group, Inc. (CRG), Merrill
Lynch Executive Compensation Group, and
Retirement Capital Group, Inc. (RCG).

With a $3,000 loan from the bank,
MacDonald launched his career as an
entrepreneur, hired his first employee, and
set out to raise the bar on financial services.
By applying the concepts outlined in this
book, MacDonald built CRG into one of
the leading executive compensation and benefits firms in the nation.

By 1999, CRG grew to 190 professionals, managed billions of dollars in assets, and maintained nine offices nationwide. Ready for new
challenges, MacDonald sold CRG to Clark Consulting, a NYSE firm,
and assumed the role of CEO for its Executive Benefits Group. He later
left to launch RCG in 2003, creating another market leader in executive
compensation and benefits.

MacDonald's latest company, PleinAire Strategies, LLC, is devoted to teaching and sharing the simplicity and effectiveness of his MERGE Process with business and academic communities.

Quoted frequently in the *Wall Street Journal,* the *New York Times, Bloomberg,* and leading trade journals, MacDonald also authored *Retain Key Executives,* a breakthrough compendium on the recruit-retain-reward challenge, published by CCH. He often lectures at the Conference Board, World-at-Work, Forbes CEO Forum and the Young Presidents' Organization. His awards include Entrepreneur of the Year and California Veteran of the Year.

MacDonald is a longtime contributor to the Million Dollar Round Table and Top of the Table organizations. A graduate of Northeastern University, he also graduated from The President's Program on Leadership (PPL) from the Harvard Business School.

Today, MacDonald regularly consults with major financial services firms on sales and marketing strategies and with key executives and boards of Fortune 500 firms, mid-size and major public and privately-held firms to improve standards of performance in the marketing and sales profession.

APPENDIX

Sample Engagement Letter

January 1, 20xx

Executive
Vice President
ABC Company, Inc.
Main Street
Anytown, CA 12345

RE: Proposed Consulting Engagement

Dear Mr. Vice President,

We appreciate the time you and your colleagues have spent with us detailing ABC's current needs and issues. We have given considerable thought to your challenge of effectively attracting and retaining key employees to support the company's growth plans. This proposal includes our strategy to develop a nonqualified deferred compensation plan that will help you meet your growth objectives. Our proposal presents our understanding of your situation, our process and fees for developing the appropriate plan for you, our qualifications for supporting you, and the benefits you will gain from our participation in this process.

UNDERSTANDING ABC COMPANY'S NEEDS

Over the past five years, ABC Company has increased revenues by 25%, primarily by opening new stores throughout the country and as a result, ABC Company has become the market leader in the retail industry. To continue this growth, you indicated the company's goal for 2011 through 2013 is to open 150 new core locations, as well as 25 super store concepts. Historically, the challenge has been attracting and retaining qualified individuals to manage these operations.

With the current 300 stores, and the 15% turnover rate among managers, you will need to recruit 246 new managers over the next three years. You indicated that through promotions you could fill 80 positions for the core stores, but you will have to look outside for the super stores, as there is a significant difference in the experience required. You also indicated that it would take a special package to recruit super store managers, as it would be difficult to find those candidates within the company.

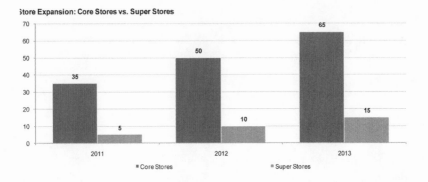

Store Expansion: Core Stores vs. Super Stores

As we discussed, turnover is a costly issue for ABC Corp. The cost of hiring and training a new manager is $55,000. The current 15% turnover in 2011 alone will cost the company $2.8 million. If the turnover percentage continues unabated ABC will have a total cost of $10 million through 2013.

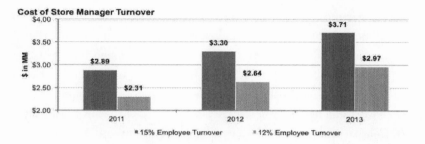

ABC can save approximately $3 million over the next three years by reducing turnover 20% (down to 12%). With average profits being $220,000 per store, hiring the right managers could increase ABC's profits by over $30 million for the core stores alone.

Undoubtedly, these turnover issues have contributed to ABC's increased store operating cost, a major factor in the total cost of company operations. Unaddressed, this continued situation could put ABC's operating objectives in at risk even to the extent of jeopardizing your status as a premier retail organization.

Recognizing these threats and opportunities for growth, your management group has suggested several options for increasing sales growth through recruitment and retention of managers, but little agreement exists about a plan that could achieve the company's goals. However, consensus does exist in two areas: the plan needs to be performance based and it must have a vesting schedule to help drive increased retention of high performing contributors.

Management must carefully develop a thorough, convincing, and comprehensive plan that is accepted by both ABC's Executive Committee and its board of directors. The plan should, at a minimum, address these questions:

- Based on the company's growth plan, how much performance measurement needs to be built into the plan?
- Should we reward for store growth or company growth or some combination?
- Should cash and/or company stock be used as the reward?
- Can we use any of our current programs as part of the reward?

To answer questions like these, ABC needs a process that will enable management to select the most effective plan to improve retention and help recruit new managers. This plan must consider not only quantitative factors (e.g. return on investment, investment incentives, taxes, and store operating expense) but also consider qualitative factors such as work force characteristics, productivity, risk, controllability, ability to develop and promote employees, and flexibility to react to unanticipated changes. Consequently, ABC needs a senior, multifaceted consulting team with a broad range of business capabilities that should include skills in strategy, compensation, tax, accounting, human resources and financial analysis. These capabilities are necessary to ensure that all relevant options are surfaced and evaluated in a practical manner, that the most desirable options and their attributes are clearly identified and defined, and that ABC's management not only has the tools to make the right decision, but that ABC is convinced of its appropriateness.

To ensure that all relevant issues are addressed in this complex engagement, the study's process should encourage a close working relationship between ABC and the consulting team. This relationship will expedite the retrieval, development, and analysis of relevant information, thus reducing the time for examination. It will also enhance the abilities of ABC's staff, producing a more capable internal team with a better appreciation of business trade-offs and broader knowledge of company operations. This broader perspective will prove helpful as business conditions change in unpredictable ways.

After carefully considering ABC's needs, my colleagues and I at XYZ Benefits have designed a process that will not only develop a recruiting and retention strategy, but also a concrete plan for implementing that strategy to improve your competitive position.

PROJECT TEAM

To ensure that ABC's managers have an integral and significant role in this engagement, we propose forming a joint ABC/XYZ Benefits team. Team members from XYZ Benefits have multi-disciplined skills in tax, accounting, legal, financial analysis and human resources. Working with ABC executives with some of these same functional skills, we will make considerable use of ABC's own market forecast and other in-house analysis. ABC's plan design team will be responsible for clarifying corporate objectives as well as making decisions on plan design, security, and funding issues that would be subject to management and Board approval.

PROJECT SCOPE AND DELIVERABLES

XYZ Benefits has created a consulting process to assist clients in developing a plan that meets their objectives. Early in the engagement we will solicit and obtain an agreement on quantitative and qualitative criteria for evaluating the various options, and throughout the engagement the team will conduct meetings to review programs and agree on future direction and emphasis. As a result of these frequent progress reviews, ABC's management will be fully informed of the engagement's ongoing findings and conclusions. The progress reviews play a key role in expediting the conduct of the engagement enabling management to keep our efforts focused by providing direction and counsel.

The team's major goal is twofold:

- To provide ABC with a recruitment and retention plan for store managers that is thoroughly documented, cost effective, and, when fully implemented, enables for the efficient recruiting and retention of managers to maintain and enhance its competitive position.
- To produce for ABC's Executive Committee and board of directors a convincing, comprehensive, and economic justification for the program.

Ideally, the output of this effort will not only be a report of the recommended plan but an actual proposal to the board of directors that justifies the cost by articulating the compelling reasons to move forward with the recommended program. To achieve this, XYZ Benefits has developed a process.

This process encompasses four disciplines for developing an effective plan:

1. Consulting
2. Funding / Asset Management
3. Communication and Education
4. Plan Administration

STEP 1: CONSULTING/PLAN DESIGN

XYZ Benefits will meet with the ABC team to review plan objectives and to address basic plan design issues. This is the listening stage where we ask questions in an effort to understand your company's goals and objectives so that they can be incorporated into the proposed plan design. These meetings will cover the following topics:

- Discussion of current company objectives. Our recommendations will be designed to benefit the selected key employees as well as enhance ABC Company's ability to achieve certain business and financial objectives. At the onset, we would help ABC Company identify and refine what it hopes to accomplish through its nonqualified deferred compensation plans.
- Education on the funding vehicles and funding issues related to nonqualified plans. The funding vehicles that can drive the decisions made by ABC Company are very important to plan participants and the overall plan cost to the company.
- Evaluate benefit security devices and develop a risk/reward analysis in examining security trusts.
- Evaluate various plan designs to meet the company's goals and do some preliminary financial analysis.

Once we have struck a proper balance between plan design, funding and security priority, the ABC / XYZ Benefits team will select among alternatives that best for achieving the company goals.

STEP 2: ASSET MANAGEMENT

One of the most important aspects of a well-designed nonqualified deferred compensation plan is the selection and management of the funding vehicle. During this step XYZ Benefits will work with ABC Company's finance department to select the funding vehicle that will properly hedge the growth of the deferred compensation plan balance. It will be necessary for the company to strike a balance between various funding priorities, such as:

- Cost of money and tax implications
- Internal rate of return
- Cash flow over the next five to seven years
- Balance sheet effects
- Cash flow during participant's distribution years

STEP 3: COMMUNICATION AND EDUCATION

XYZ Benefits excels at educating plan participants through personalized information and interaction. Participants can access plan information through a secure website, or with the help of the Client Service Team Representatives from XYZ Benefits. Our education curriculum addresses the specific needs of your employees by communicating throughout their employment cycle: prior to eligibility, during enrollment, throughout the vesting period of the retention plan, and through the post-vesting period of the retention plan.

XYZ Benefits will develop a customized communication strategy to determine the appropriate education material based on your goals. We incorporate a range of customized and personalized communications across multiple media formats, including:

- Communication strategy development
- Onsite and webcast education sessions
- Ongoing monitoring of communication strategy

Step 4: Administration

Nonqualified plans require varying degrees of third-party plan administration. XYZ Benefits will coordinate any plan changes and provide enrollment and plan communications to the participants of both plans. As part of plan administration, we will provide periodic financial reports to help you effectively manage the unique reporting requirements of nonqualified plans. XYZ Benefits can supplement any additional reporting requirements you may require. We will review the following financial reporting package with ABC Company's finance and accounting departments:

- Plan Asset reports
- Plan Liability reports
- Budget projection
- Other ad-hoc financial project reports

Monitoring / Continuous Services

XYZ Benefits provides value for the life of a plan, continually reviewing the administration platform offerings to make sure our clients receive the highest quality service. We also continue to consult with the company on changes in the law, best practices, and other elements that will impact your plan in the long run. XYZ Benefits is organized through our consulting teams to continue to assist ABC Company in the annual enrollment process and review of the plan.

Timetable

Ideally, the output of this effort will not only be a report of the recommended plan but an actual proposal to Corporate that justifies the cost by articulating the compelling reasons to move forward quickly.

Please note this three month estimate for completing the first two steps in the study is conservative. Working with your management team, we will make every effort to accelerate the completion of the tasks. The following is our initial timetable:

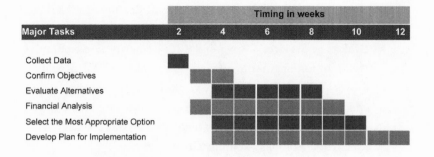

Major Tasks	Timing in weeks					
	2	4	6	8	10	12
Collect Data						
Confirm Objectives						
Evaluate Alternatives						
Financial Analysis						
Select the Most Appropriate Option						
Develop Plan for Implementation						

Project Outline and Fees

- **Timetable** – Subject to the timely receipt of required information from ABC Company and the availability of your team for
  meeting purposes; we believe Steps 1 through 4 can be completed
  in approximately 60 days.
- **Professional Fees** – Our consulting fees for Steps 1 and 2 is
  **$3,000, with 50% paid at the beginning of the project and the
  balance upon XYZ Benefits' satisfactory completion of Steps 1
  and 2.** Any outside legal, tax, or account review at your request is
  separate from our fees and would be determined by you with the
  outside advisors. XYZ Benefits will present proven best practices
  strategies that comply with current legislation.
- **Out-of-Pocket Expenses** – ABC Company agrees to reimburse
  XYZ Benefits for its reasonable actual out-of-pocket expenses
  incurred in connection with this engagement. Out-of-pocket
  expenses may include but are not limited to those beyond XYZ
  Benefits' normal general office chares for telephone calls, faxing,
  word processing, secretarial, overnight delivery, printing, tele-
  copying, mileage, or other travel (within a fifty-five mile radius of
  the corporate headquarters).
- **Communication, Education, and Administration** (Steps 3 and
  4) – Implementation, enrollment, and communication will not
  have additional fees unless ABC Company requests a new service
  or additional resources that are not presently known, or we are
  not designated as brokers of record. Administration fees charged

by XYZ Benefits will be quoted separately. Revenue sharing should be available from the funding assets to offset some of this cost.

- **Brokerage Services** – Assuming ABC Company elects to implement our funding recommendations by utilizing XYZ Benefits as brokers, XYZ Benefits will receive product-based compensation which will be fully disclosed under our transparency policies. As discussed above, some of the revenue sharing will also help to lower ABC Company administration costs.

ABOUT XYZ BENEFITS, LLC

XYZ Benefits is committed to helping companies attract, reward, and retain their talented and most valued employees through our consultative process, which is executed by a team of specialists in the field of nonqualified plan design. This experience provides XYZ Benefits with a competitive advantage in the marketplace.

The XYZ Benefits team is also experienced in a number of benefit disciplines; including those who have practiced as tax and ERISA attorneys, CPAs, financial analysts, and actuaries. We leverage these experts to maintain a consistent high standard of quality. We bring a comprehensive platform of products and tools to deliver a customized nonqualified plan solution.

XYZ's focus is to provide clients with comprehensive solutions encompassing all aspects of plan design, securitization, funding, implementation, and administration of key employee benefit programs.

We believe that XYZ Benefits is uniquely qualified to provide ABC Company with the key employee benefit consulting services it requires now, and in the future.

CONFIDENTIALITY

It is understood that in providing these services XYZ Benefits may receive confidential and proprietary business and/or personal information of both ABC Company and individual employees of ABC Company and agrees not to disclose such information to any third party without the prior written consent of ABC Company. In the event that such third party disclosure is consented to, XYZ Benefits shall communicate the confidential and proprietary nature of the information to such third parties and use best efforts to ensure that such third parties treat such information as confidential.

STAFFING

I will personally lead this project with the assistance of our lead consultant and our internal design team and technical staff. In addition, we will add a dedicated client service team to assist us with implementation and administration. XYZ Benefits professionals have extensive experience in designing and implementing plans for some of the largest companies in the country. We have worked with several organizations that share the same objectives as ABC Company.

SUMMARY

If you are in agreement with the process described above, along with the terms and conditions contained in this correspondence, and desire to engage our services, please sign, date, and return a copy of this letter at your earliest convenience.

Thank you again for the opportunity to share this information with you. Please call me if you have any questions regarding this letter or if you would like additional information regarding our consulting practice.

Sincerely,
William MacDonald
President & CEO
Approved and Agreed to:

By: _____

Title: _____

Date: _____, 2011

Appendix II

Letter to the Shareholders

Dear Shareholders,

When I decided to join Company ABC nearly five years ago, I looked at this business as any investor would. What was clear to me from the beginning was that we had talented people and a strong niche in the retail marketplace. At the same time, we had an incredible opportunity to transform Company ABC from a good company to a world-class organization.

We set out looking at our business in new ways *[Looking at business in new ways]*, challenging how we operate and our assumptions about what our clients expect. We cast aside a "business as usual" approach, knowing that in retail if you are not changing or reinventing your business constantly, you run the risk of losing ground with your client. We reviewed all aspects of our strategy and business processes *[Review strategy and business process]*. We worked diligently to test, learn, and develop a long-range plan for our business *[Long range plan]*. We focused on creating shareholder value through programs to improve merchandising, marketing, and store-level performance, supplemented by diligent and strict expense control *[Creating shareholder value]*. We committed to healthy growth, and we said we would not grow the store base until *[Grow stores in profitable manor]*. we could assure you that we were doing so in a profitable manner These strategies and disciplines are now deeply embedded in our culture *[Deeply embedded in culture]* and have served us well. We have grown our operating profit from $27 million in 2005 to over $325 million in 2009 — a year that will likely go down as one of the most difficult environments in retail history. And along the way, we have generated nearly $1.2 billion of cash, the majority of which we have returned to you, our shareholders, in the form of share repurchase activity *[Buying back shares with cash they have generated. How can we show the economics of our plan improving the company's P&L compared to buying shares back?]*.

I am very proud of the team's effort [Team]. During this past year, when the global recession took its toll on the market and economic news turned morning coffee bitter:

- We completed our 3rd consecutive year of record EPS performance, a span that now dates back 13 consecutive quarters. *[EBS growth and record profits]*
- We generated record operating profit dollars of over $325 million.
- We grew our store base for the first time since 2004 by opening more stores in 2009 than we have in the last 3 years combined. *[Growing store base —how will they hire people from this growth? Do they promote from within? Do they have a management training program?]*
- We invested in new systems and put capital to work in our business and fleet of stores to enhance the client experience.
- And, in a world where cash is king, we generated over $300 million in cash. *[They have lots of cash so we should discuss earnings per share (EPS) and how to deploy the cash to improve economics]*
- Our Board of Directors has authorized the repurchase of up to $400 million of our common shares. *[Repurchasing stock]*

In the balance of this letter, I will detail some of the significant 2009 highlights, and also lay out for you some of our thoughts on the future and our plans for continuing to enhance shareholder value *[He is going to give us his vision and strategy for the future]*.

Our business has generated a significant amount of cash in recent years. My job as CEO is to ensure we are investing your cash in the opportunities that we expect to generate strong returns, whether that is in our existing concepts or new strategies *[He wants to invest the company's cash to improve the value of shareholders. Back to showing how EPS can be improved with our solutions. He is open to "new strategies"]*. I have said on a number of occasions that we have "an open to receive" and would look at any opportunity to drive profitable growth and shareholder value *[Look at any opportunity to drive profitability]*. Looking forward to 2010 and beyond, we believe the best opportunity (internal or external) is to reinvest in our current locations and grow our fleet of stores profitably.

Clearly our business model has gotten stronger each year, and we are confident in our plans heading into 2010. Additionally, the difficulties experienced in the economy have taken their toll on retailers and the commercial real estate market. As a result, today there are fewer retailers vying for locations and, in our estimation, real estate prices are becoming more appropriately valued in the marketplace *[If I were in the commercial real estate business, this would be key]*. The combination of our improved performance and a softer real estate market enabled us to move into a store growth mode again in 2009. And the good news is we see that rate of growth accelerating in 2010 and future years *[Projecting real growth]*. The soft real estate market also enabled us to make progress in lease renegotiations as stores came up for renewal with landlords who saw their retail vacancies soar during the recession. These renegotiations have helped us keep costs in check or rise at a lower rate than the lease would have otherwise indicated.

We were also very busy testing two specific, new real estate strategies in 2009: "A" locations and a smaller store strategy *[Good to understand their growing strategy for increasing the number of stores]*.

- The "A" location test started with 8 stores in higher than average income areas or in locations with a better cotenant mix or both. Our key learning was, with great value in merchandising, improved visual presentation, and higher in-store execution standards, we can perform very well in "A" locations. We are moving forward aggressively on this strategy by planning to open approximately 30 "A" locations in 2010. We believe this could be a very big win for the business by expanding our client base and improving our overall level of brand awareness for the future *[Opening 30 "A" locations which might take a different talent to run. He sees opening these stores as a "very big win." It sounds like they're "testing" of the market sees more potential with "A" stores versus the smaller store strategy.]*

- With our smaller store strategy test in 3 locations, the results to date have been somewhat mixed, and it is still too early to make a determination. We will make adjustments to this strategy in 2010 and continue to monitor the results. The idea remains intriguing to us and if successful, could open up a significant number of additional sites that we could consider for future growth.

I feel good about our direction in real estate, and I am confident it is the best investment we can be making right now for the future of the company. Going forward, store growth will be a principle priority for our team *["Store growth is a principal priority for our team"]*.

Like any retailer, merchandising and having the "right stuff" for the client is crucial to our success. Over the last 4 years, we have made a concerted effort to merchandise the store with better quality product and more recognizable brand names. We have aggressively pursued new vendor relationships while enhancing the value proposition across our store. In fact, in the last 2 years, we have added well over 1,000 new vendors *[Who are the new vendor relationships? Are any of these clients of ours?]*. With a deeper vendor base, the availability of deals and inventory at extreme value remains vibrant, and it's the merchandising team's job to make the tough choice on which item to choose and how many to buy. I am proud of the merchant team and how well inventory was managed in 2009, which resulted in a record inventory turnover rate for this business.

Over the past 2 years, I believe that we have seen a permanent shift in client demand toward greater value and saving money. We have encouraged our merchants to enhance our value proposition to be even more competitive in order to give our clients the kinds of savings they need during these challenging economic times *[This would be an opportunity for us to say something like, "Like you, over the past few years our clients have been demanding greater value and want to reduce cost." With that we… we could add how we can enhance their cost, improve their EPS, or attract and retain people that can "enhance their client's value"].* With better-planned and better presented merchandise up and down our aisles, we have seen our clients respond and our average transaction size increase. From home and consumables to furniture, toys, electronics, and seasonal, we continue to offer our clients more brand names and better quality goods at unmatched prices.

Innovative programs to improve the client experience as well as the shop-ability and appearance of our stores are key elements of our strategic plan. Specifically, in 2009, we launched our Ready for Business initiative across our entire fleet of over 1,360 stores. Ready for Business is a multi-year initiative focused on executing well-defined, chainwide standards that enhance the vitality of our inventory and place a greater emphasis on the client shopping experience *[Always look for initiatives and see if you can write them in your reports and proposals. Also, use them in your meetings. The "Ready for Business" initiative is important to them. How can we measure this and reward store owners through our programs].*

Much like our efforts to control costs, we should always be challenging ourselves to get better on the sales floor *[Another area to reward for].* As an example, our Food Refresh Program was completed in 2009 and is part of our in-store strategy to improve the shopability of the food department, one of the largest volume areas of our stores. This initiative focused on elevating cleanliness and presentation requirements, training associates *[Find out if this is what they call their employees. If so, use associates vs. employees in all your materials]* who are responsible for this area, introducing new freshness guaranteed marketing and, in over half of our stores, investing capital in new fixtures.

In order to execute to a better, more consistent in-store standard, we have also been making a meaningful investment in our people and attracting new talent over the last year *[Perfect—they "have also been making a meaningful investment in our people and attracting new talent over the last year." Ask them how they've been doing this.].* Given our recent financial performance, we have become an employer of choice in the marketplace and have been able to recruit new talent at the store, district, and regional vice president levels *["Employer of Choice" therefore they may be very interested in peer analysis or some benchmarking. Find out where the new talent has been coming from. Look on LinkedIn to see where new hires have come from.].* In 2009, we launched our Leadership Institute—an intensive management development program for District Managers who were new to the organization or were being promoted from within the organization *[Another opportunity around management development etc. Ask them to tell you more about this as it may open up opportunities to discuss how you can help them attract, retain and reward these district managers. Also gives you an opportunity to discuss their organizational structure]*—to develop leaders for our future.

Technology remains an important strategic imperative at Company ABC, both to strengthen connections with our clients and to improve our processes. This year we launched our rewards program *[Another opportunity the rewards program He mentions this is a "key initiative to growing transactions and expanding our current client base." How can we design something that can get store managers and district managers to focus on this?].* This effort represents our first loyalty card program which will allow us to learn more about our clients' buying habits, encourage more frequent visits, and/or potentially expand our client base. We are encouraged about the progress to date and have enrolled well over 1.5 million members. Our data suggest these new rewards members are spending more than double what the average client spends, and in stores with the highest number of rewards members, we are experiencing measurable increases in transactions. In 2010, we will invest further in technology to provide us with the tools necessary to begin to directly market to our rewards members based on their specific buying patterns and history. We see the rewards program, along with our focus on improving the in-store shopping experience, as two key initiatives to growing transactions and expanding our current client base.

Beyond our strategies, over 35,000 Company ABC associates *[They do call employees "associates"]* are dedicated to doing more to serve our clients. As part of our mission, we encourage every member of our team to develop strong bonds in the communities where we live and work *[How do they do this? How do they measure and do they reward for this?].* We will continue to be committed to making a difference to those we serve by stocking food banks, supporting volunteerism, and donating hundreds of thousands of dollars to schools, social service agencies, and local and national charities.

As CEO, it has been my personal mission to ensure that constant change remains a vital part of our culture *[They believe in continuous improvement]*. And I can assure you the spirit of innovation is alive and well at Company ABC.

Our ability to embrace change—to reinvent ourselves—has been key to our success to date. We are passionate about accomplishment and accountability *[All key, you need to use these words back in your proposals and reports]*. Our desire to deliver outstanding performance is matched by a determination to respond to new realities. Our results demonstrate that Company ABC is a robust and growing business that is capable of performing in both good times and tough times. I am confident we are well positioned as we begin 2010, and we have a solid business plan in place that balances the need for results today with a focus on tomorrow.

I have been with Company ABC coming up on 5 years this summer, and I firmly believe that heading into 2010 we are better positioned than at any other time in my tenure with the Company. Our merchandise content and the value message continue to grow stronger and stronger, our stores have never looked better, inventories are flowing and well under control, and we continue to find smart ways to leverage our cost structure without impacting the client *[Again, they are focused on cost and improving.]*. For 2010, we have provided financial guidance that forecasts our 4th consecutive year of record EPS from continuing operations, accelerates store growth, generates significant cash flow, and will return a minimum of $150 million to shareholders in the form of share repurchase activity.

I feel very comfortable with how we have planned 2010; however, I am more excited when I think about the opportunities for this business longer term. As a management team, we are focused on strategies and initiatives to drive continued growth over the next several years *[Management teams focus]*. Earlier this year, we communicated to the marketplace a view of the next three years … 2010 through 2012. By 2012, we believe sales could exceed $5.5 billion with an operating profit rate of 8% *[Could factor this in as a measurement for reward, tied with a retention of key management talent.*

You should look at the proxy statement under the recommendation table and see if this is a part of any of their bonus plans, etc.] and EPS from continuing operations approaching $3.50 per diluted share. This model would generate $650 million to $700 million of cash while continuing to invest for the future and grow our store base. Over the next 3 years alone, we expect to add a net of approximately 140 stores, which creates hundreds of opportunities for promotions for our best performers and potentially creates in the neighborhood of 4,000 to 5,000 jobs to do our part to help the economy grow and improve the overall employment picture *[Key for attracting and retaining key people. Question you could ask "with an aggressive plan to add 140 stores over the next three years, where will the talent come from? How many internal promotions, etc? Retaining rising starts will be important."]*.

In my estimation, the future for this Company has never been brighter. Our model and execution continue to get stronger and stronger. We have entered into a growth mode *[Growth mode]* which is the next phase of our evolution. And with the potential for a store base of over 2,000 stores, I see this as a 9 or 10 billion dollar business, or nearly double the size that it is today.

On behalf of our Board of Directors, I would like to thank you—our community of shareholders, clients, vendors, and suppliers—for your ongoing support. And to all of our associates and their families, I offer my deepest thanks and appreciation for the hard work and commitment you give to our company every day.

Sincerely,
Company ABC
Chairman, CEO and President

INDEX